History Today

Indian History and Culture Society

B-17, Qutab Institutional Area, New Delhi - 110 016

History Today

Journal of the Indian History and Culture Society

No. 4 2003

Editor

Vandana Kaushik

Assistant Editor

Anuja Geetali

D.K. Printworld (P) Ltd.
New Delhi

Cataloging in Publication Data — DK
[Courtesy: D.K. Agencies (P) Ltd. <docinfo@dkagencies.com>]

History today : Journal of the Indian History and Culture Society, no. 4, 2003 / editor, Vandana Kaushik ; assistant editor, Anuja Geetali.
viii, 104 p. 28 cm.
Reprint.
Includes bibliographical references.
ISBN 8124604517

1. India — History — Periodicals. 2. India — Social conditions — Periodicals. 3. Ayodhya (India) — Antiquities — Periodicals. 4. Temples, Hindu — India — History — Periodicals. 5. Islam — India — History — Periodicals. 6. Cities and towns — India — Growth — History — Periodicals. I. Kaushik, Vandana. II. Geetali, Anuja

DDC 954.005 22

ISBN 81-246-0451-7
First Published in India in 2003
Reprinted in 2008

History Today, no. 4 (2003) Rs. 500 **$ 25.00**

Reprint authorised by
Indian History and Culture Society, New Delhi - 110016

Manuscripts (Whether in the form of aricles or notes or book reviews) offered for publcation, should be sent to the Editor, History Today, Indian History and Culture Society, B-17, Qutab Institutional Area, New Delhi-110016.

Published and printed by:
D.K. Printworld (P) Ltd.
Regd. office : *'Sri Kunj,'* F-52, Bali Nagar
Ramesh Nagar Metro Station
New Delhi - 110 015
Phones : (011) 2545 3975, 2546 6019; *Fax* : (011) 2546 5926
E-mail : dkprintworld@vsnl.net
Web : www.dkprintworld.com

History Today

Contents

Editorial

History Today is committed to fulfill the aims and objectives of the Indian History and Culture Society. It has provided a forum for those scholars and historians, who believe in the cause of history and value true representation of facts.

The article 'Islam and Islamic Iconoclasm in India', asserts the fact that Islam in India is not what orthodox section of its followers want people to believe. In fact, Indian Islam is Indianized to a great extent and according to the author Aurangazeb acted in un-Islamic manner.

This issue has articles mainly on regional history covering its different aspects like social history, religious history and art history. Temple patronage in early medieval Rajasthan, a result of changes in political, economic and religious relations is reflected in the article, 'Rulers, Urban Milieu and Temple Patronage: Shifting Countours in Rajasthan'. This study is based mainly on inscriptional data. The paper on *Biḍāla-nrisiṁha* Temple near Sambalpur, Orissa brings out the emergence of a syncretic cult in the form of Biḍālanrisiṁha, a unique temple where the image of Nrisiṁha has face of a cat and the body of a lion. An article on the Aḷvar Movements in Kerala discusses about the impact of Vaishnava Movement on the culture of Kerala mainly in the form of structural temples and festivals of *Vishu* and *Onam*. The growth of medieval cities and towns is described in the article 'Pattern of Urban Growth in Northern India in the Sixteenth and Seventeenth Centuries'. '*Tawaif* and *khawas* in the Hyderabad State' is a study through gender perspective. Sikh Gurus rejected the caste discrimination, this fact is highlighted in the article, 'Rejection of Caste Inequalities by the Sikh Gurus'. The paper on Kanhoji Angre, based on the primary sources proves that he was the virtual master of Konkan waters in the Arabian Sea in the late 17th century. This issue also includes one paper which was circulated in the media, about the excavations at Ayodhya and three articles by leading archeologists and historians of Medieval India, which clear all misconceptions regarding the findings of the excavations.

This issue is quite comprehensive as it has papers on the history of Punjab, Orissa, Kerala, Rajasthan, Hyderabad and Konkan. Thus almost all the parts of the country are represented through these articles.

Notes, News and New Source Material column features a new discovery of a circular temple similar to that of Ayodhya type excavated at Kashipur. Recent findings at Hathab, an early historic site of Gujrat are also included in this volume.

We are grateful to the scholars and publishers who have sent us their books for review.

We are thankful to Dr. S. P. Gupta and Shri K. N. Dikshit for their continuous support and guidance. Thanks are also due to Dr. Saroj Gulati who helped us in many ways. We are also thankful to our young scholars, Ms. Sonali Gupta and Shri T. Arun Raj who unhesitatingly helped us.

We express our sincere thanks to the Indian Council of Historical Research for the financial assistance which has helped us to publish this journal in the present form.

The editors of this journal are not responsible for the opinions expressed by the authors whose articles, notes, reviews etc., have been published in this issue.

Thanks are also due to Mrs. Anita Mehta and her staff for bringing out this journal in time.

Vandana Kaushik

Islam and Islamic Iconoclasm in India

R. Nath*

Islam was born in the 7th century A.D., in primitive desert conditions of Arabia, essentially, as a socio-religious reformatory movement, to 'civilize' the Bedouin Arabs who were hitherto living in'ignorance' (*jahilijah jahlat*). The Quran, its sacred book, also called *al-kitab*, was deemed to be the word of God (kalamu'llah), revealed to the Prophet Muhammed through the angel Gabriel (Ar. Jibre'il or Jibril). It is in Arabic and it was meant for the Arabic people. This has been stressed by Allah himself in the Quran several times, e.g.,

'We have sent it down
as an Arabic Quran,
In order that ye may
learn wisdom' (XII.2; *HQ*.550)[1]

There are numerous other references in Quran itself (e.g. XIII.37; XVI.103; XX.113; XXVI.192-195; XXXIX.28; XLI.3; XLI.44; XLII.7; XLIII.3; XLVI.12 and so on) (besides numerous others in the *Hadiths* or traditions or sayings of the prophet and his companions) which uphold the concept of an Arabic Quran and show that Islam, in its origin, had no world view, and its idea of *Dar'ul-Islam* (the World of Islam) was originally limited to the *Hijaz* (the region of Mecca and Madina) or, at the most, Arabia, inhabited by tribes who spoke Arabic.

The Quran chapter-XIV verse 4 (*HQ*, 620) specifically ordained:

'We sent not an apostle
except (to teach) in the language
of his (own people, in order
to make (things) clear to them.'

And confirmed unequivocally, that Islam was meant only for the Arabs, and not for those whose mother tongue was not Arabic.

The Quran

The Quran has 6239 verses in 114 chapters *(surahs)*, practically covering all the subjects related to the contemporary society: socio-economic and political as well as religio-philosophical, mostly in the form of injunctions laying down foundations of Islam which was as much a law as a Faith. The Quran was not compiled in the Prophet's life-time, and it was only after his death (in 632 A.D.) that the first *Khalifah* (successor, vice-regent) Abu Bakr (632-34) ordered Zaid ibn Sabit, the Prophet' s own secretary, to compile it. He collected verses from palm-leaves, tablets

*Former Professor & Head of History Dept., Rajasthan University, Jaipur

of white stone and memory, and a text was prepared. There were variants and Usman, the third Khalifa (644-56) set up in 651 A.D., a committee of knowledgeable persons with the same Zaid as its chairman, for its revision, authentication and finalisation, on the basis of Abu Bakr's copy. After thorough collation, scrutiny and deliberations, a standard text of the Quran was prepared. Its three copies were made. The original was kept at Madina and the copies were sent to Damascus, Basrah and Kufah, the three upcoming centres of Islam. All other copies were destroyed and this became the standard, perfect and invariable text of the Quran in which no change, even that of a comma, was hereafter permitted.

It is important to note that these verses were revealed in accordance with the exigency of the occasion in each case, and each and every verse had a context, without which it cannot be understood. There is absolutely no doubt that verses of the Quran were meticulously examined by the Zaid committee which comprised of contemporaries who had lived with the Prophet and who personally knew their contents, and it was after complete authentication that the verses were included in the standard text. There is no possibility of interpolation of any spurious verse (by the Satan, the Devil, or anybody else) which, in any case, could not have escaped the notice of the learned 'editors' of the Zaid committee who, on discovery of any such spurious verse, could not have allowed it to be included in the standard text. As such, the doctrine of abrogation of verses (*mansuk* or cancellation) has no merit. It is a later interpretation to explain the contradictions which occurred in several instances. Allah has himself stated in the Quran on this subject decisively:

> 'None of our revelations do we abrogate
> Or cause to be forgotten, but we substitute
> Something better or similar: Knowest thou not that God
> Hath power over all things?' (II.106, *HQ*, 46-47).

There cannot be any such distinction as Divine verses and satanic verses of the Quran, and such a distinction, and preference to certain verses to the abrogation of others, was made by the later theologians for their own convenience, in accordance with the prevalent socio-political conditions.

Islamic Law of Peaceful Co-Existence

The prophet was at war with the Pagan Meccans and the Jews who refused to accept him and, there is no doubt that, there were instances of massacre and arson, as usually happened in wars in medieval times. But he was making a civilization out of barbarism, and a state out of tribal anarchy. He wanted to live, even with his non-believing compatriots, with peace and amity. His Islam did not ordain to use force in religious matters, and the Quranic injunction against use of force in religion is specific and unambiguous:

> 'Let there be no compulsion in religion: Truth stands out
> Clear from Error: whoever rejects Evil and believes
> In God hath grasped the most trustworthy
> Hand-hold, that never breaks. And God heareth
> And Knoweth all things.' (II.256, *HQ*,103).

It laid down the principle that compulsion is incompatible, with religion because religion depends upon faith and will, and these will be meaningless if induced by force.

There is a full chapter in the Quran entitled: '*kafirun*' or those who reject faith, which contains a more specific and assertive injunction in this respect:

1. 'I say: o ye that reject faith
2. I worship not that which ye worship
3. Nor will ye worship, that which I worship,
4. And I will not worship that which ye have been-want to worship,
5. Nor will ye worship, that which I worship
6. To you be your way, and to me mine.' (CIX. I-6, *HQ*, 1800).

This established the principle of toleration and peaceful co-existence of the Muslim state with its non-believing subjects.

It was, in fact, on these foundations that Islamic Civilization was built, in place of pre-Islamic barbarism.

'Jaziyah' and 'Jihad'

The Quran laid down, unambiguously, that the Muslim state cannot be at war with its own non-believing subjects if they paid a nominal poll-tax called 'jaziyah' (which means compensation), e .g.

> 'Fight those who believe not, in God nor the Last Day,
> Nor hold that forbidden which hath been forbidden
> By God and His Apostle, nor acknowledge the Religion
> Of Truth (even if they are) of the People of the Book,
> Until they pay the *Jizyah* with willing submission,
> And feel themselves subdued'(IX.29, *HQ,* 447).

Payment of '*Jaziyah*' by the non-believers cast upon the Muslim State a '*zimmah*' or contract, covenant, treaty, liability or obligation, to protect their (1) life (2) property and (3) religion, and (4) exempt them from military service. They are called *Zimmis* (or the protected people) and *Jaziyah* entitled and enabled them to live under the protection of the state for saving their personal liberty of conscience, and this was the primary condition of '*jaziyah*'. In other words, it was paid to the state in lieu of this protection and, as sanctioned by the Quran, it was a sort of contract between the State and its people, like the '*mahr*' which was a contract between the husband and wife. The Injunction of '*jihad*' (the holy or religious war) , as propounded in such verses of the Quran as 11.216-217 (*HQ,* 84-85); IV.74-76 (*HQ,* 202); VIII.39 (*HQ,* 424) and IX.4-6 (HQ, 439-440) for example, was meant for the Pagans of Mecca and was of local implication only, in accordance with the exigency of the occasion, and it was not meant for universal application in all lands, and at all times, to come, and it was not the least meant for the non-believing subjects of the Muslim state from whom not only the land-revenue (*kharaj*), but (*jaziyah*) too was collected. It was not meant, at all, to humiliate the non-believers so as to compel them to embrace Islam, as the later theologians interpreted, as Qazi Mughisuddin did to Alau'd-Din Khalji (1296-1316). Unfortunately, the *Mullas,* being the only lettered class in the Muslim society in medieval India, imposed their own perverted views upon the Muslim state in order to maintain their hold upon it, and the barbaric acts perpetrated upon the non-believers in medieval India, and masqueraded as Islamic, were, in fact, the fanatical views of the *Mullas.*

As such, if a Muslim state demolished religious shrines of the non-believers even when it collected the *Jaziyah,* besides the land-revenue (*kharaj*), like Aurangzeb who demolished temples of the Hindus ruthlessly, it acted in gross violation of the Quranic injunction, cited above, besides being guilty of breach of the *Jaziyah* contract and betrayal of the trust by its own helpless subjects reposed in it by its payment. It was not *'jihad,* it was an un-Islamic barbaric act.

Let us, therefore, make a distinction between the Prophet's Islam as expounded in the Quran, which prescribed toleration, peaceful co-existence and protection of the non-believers living in the Muslim state on payment of *jaziyah,* as cited above: and the Mulla's Islam which prescribed an uncompromising iconoclasm and total extermination of the non-believers.

'Mazar' – Worship

Several offshoots of Islam developed in India (11th to 17th century A.D.) which transgressed its basic tenets. *Mazar* worship was one such development. Several *Ahadith* (*hadiths*) prohibit building of *pucci* (masonry) graves or tombs, with stones, burnt bricks or mortar, plastering them, or decorating them with pictures or inscriptions. Thus, one recorded, Jabir said: The Prophet prohibited building with mortar on graves and also placing inscriptions upon them' (*Mishkat,* v, vi, 1). Another stated, Ali said: 'Shall I not give you the orders which the Prophet gave me, namely, to destroy all pictures and images, and not to leave a single lofty tomb without lowering it within a span from the ground' (*Muslim* II.p.459, Srl No.215)[2]. The Prophet's grave at Madina was *kachchi* (unbuilt) and was 'covered with red gravel' (*Mishkat,* v, vi, 2).

Imam Muslim, one of the six exponents of *Hadith,* expounded several other *hadiths* on this subject. One recorded, 'Aisha reported that the Prophet said: 'when a pious person amongst them (among the religious groups) dies, they build a place of worship on his grave, and then decorate it with such pictures. They would be the worst creatures on the Day of Judgment in the sight of Allah' (*Muslim,* Srl No.1076). And, 'A'isa reported that the Prophet said : 'Allah cursed the Jews and the Christians that they took the gravess of the their Prophets as mosques (places of worship). Had it been so, his (the Prophet's) grave would have been in an open place, but it could not be due to the fear that it may not be taken as a mosque '(Muslim, Srl. No .1079). And, Abu Huraira reported that the Prophet said: "Let Allah destroy the Jews for they have taken the graves of their apostles as places of worship" (Muslim, Srl No.1080). And, Fazala bin 'Ubaid said : 'I heard the Messenger of Allah commanding (us) to level grave' (Muslim, Srl No. 2114). And, Jabir said : 'Allah's messenger forbade that the graves should be plastered, or they be used as sitting places (for the people), or a building should be built over them' (Muslim, Srl NO. 2116, 2117). And, Jabir said that he was forbidden to build *'pucci'* graves (i.e. built with stone or brick masonry), indicating that the graves should be covered by earth only and left *'kachchi'* (unbuilt).

Thus, not only it was prohibited to build graves with brick or stone, any form of prayer or worship, in fact, any adoration to the grave or tomb was also forbidden. The Prophet prayed that God would not allow his followers to make his tomb an object of idolatrous adoration, because adoration shown to his tomb, in fact, to any tomb, would amount to its worship which was against the monotheistic concept of Islam: that there is no other god except Allah (which is contained in the *Kalma,* the Islamic creed itself). Idolatrous adoration, in any form was, unequivocally, forbidden in the Quran :

'Take not with God, another object of worship;
Or thou (o man) wilt sit, in disgrace and
Destitution' (XVII.22, *HQ,* 700)
And: 'Thy Lord hath decreed
That ye worship none but Him' (XVII.23, *HQ,* 700).

This also rules out reading of *Fatiha* on graves or tombs, or showing idolatrous adoration to them, in any form. *Fatiha* is the first chapter of the Quran in praise of God and his attributes:

1. 'In the name of God, Most gracious, most merciful *(Bismillah-ir-Reheman-ir-Rahim),*
2. Praise be to God, the cherisher and sustainer of the Worlds
3. Most gracious, Most merciful,
4. Master of the Day of Judgment.
5. Thee do we worship, and thine aid we seek.
6. Show us the straight way,
7. The way of those on whom thou hast bestowed thy grace, those whose (portion) is not wrath, and who go not a stray' (Quran-1, *HQ,* 14-15).

It is thus an extremely short and simple prayer. But it is usually read, in India, as an intercession for the souls of the departed, in a particular form at the graves and tombs: one stands at the foot of the grave (on its south side), facing it, with open palms, joined together, in the gesture of begging; bows in adoration; and reads *Fatiha* to invoke God's mercy. This is a ceremonial or formal act, and performed with flowers, incenses and '*chadar*' (sheet of cloth to cover the grave with reverence and devotion), for example, it is a 'ritual' and, because grave is manifestly the object of adoration, it amounts to tomb worship. *Mazhar* (Persian term denoting a holy tomb) and *dargah* (also a Persian term denoting a shrine or tomb of a *Sufi* or holy person, which is object of *ziyarat*=pilgrimage) provide free occasion for this ritual.

This is plainly against the orthodox religion of Islam. But, inspite of all the *shari'at*[3] prohibitions cited above, *mazhar*-worship is practised, freely, by the Muslim masses throughout India, with such great centres as Ajmer, Delhi, Agra and Fatehpur Sikri and Lahore. It is an Islamic form of image or icon worship of the Hindus. Though it transgresses *shari'at,* the *mullas* have no courage to raise their voice against this essentially un-Islamic practice and condemn it. They hide behind the excuse that it is just a Sufistic aberration of Islam which is tolerated owing to its mass appeal and popular approbation. Hypocrisy which breeds from cowardice is its worst form.

Islamic Iconoclasm in India

Iconoclasm: demolition of temples and desecration of images: was a similar development of Islam in India. It was perpetrated both by foreign invaders and by its own rulers, the two being quite different phenomena. Mahmud of Ghazni (reign, 997-1030 A.D.) (and other foreign invaders who followed him, down to Ahmed Shah Abdali-Durrani, mid- 18th century A.D.) destroyed temples and plundered their wealth, in the name of Islam, in spite of the Quranic injunctions (II.256 and CIX. 106, cited above). It must be noted, however, that he did not do this barbarism in his own State, but in the enemy territory, as part of the warfare, and he did not annexe the regions where temples were demolished, and he did this barbarism against the people from whom he was not collecting land-revenue (*kharaj*) or *jaziyah* or any other tax, and had, therefore, no obligation to protect them. It was obviously, the failure of the Hindu state whose liability it was to protect its own people against the barbarism of foreign invaders. Of course, it was for this protection alone that the people paid land-revenue to their king.

Also noteworthy is the fact, secondly, that Mahmud did not raise a mosque in place of the temple which he demolished for the simple reason that there was no Muslim population to use and sustain it. He left the temple in ruins and did not forcibly and illegitimately acquire and occupy its land, upon which a new temple was, subsequently, built and *puja* (worship) resummed.This aspect of Mahmud's iconoclasm is singularly important. Plain and simple, it was an act of plunder (*loot-mar*) and Islam's name was just exploited to incite his followers, mostly Afghan mercenaries, and for his own glorification in the Islamic world. His barbarism, perpetrated in the medieval ages, can thus be explained, to some extent, as an act of war.

But the iconoclasm perpetrated by its own rulers, who were born in India and whose state was collecting land-revenue (*kharaj*) and poll-tax (*jaziyah*) from the people, was altogether different. For example, Aurangzeb (reign, 1658-1707 A.D.) 'issued orders to the governors of all the provinces to demolish the schools and temples of the infidels' on 8 April 1669 and, consequently, thousands of Hindu[4] temples were razed to the ground throughout the Mughal Empire, as is graphically described by the contemporary historian Saqi Must'ad Khan in his *Ma'asir-i Alamgiri*[5]. It was in compliance of this Black Decree that the Vishwanath Temple of Kashi (Banaras) was destroyed (August-September,1669)[6] and a mosque was built in its place. In all probability, the temples of Ayodhya, including the Ram-Janmasthan Temple, in whatever form it was then existing, were also demolished in the same sequence, c.1669. The temples of the Braja region were also destroyed. The famous temple of Kesho Rai at Mathura, was demolished and a mosque was raised upon its land[7]. Saqi Must'ad Khan recorded that it was large temple, built by Bir Singh Deo Bundela at the cost of 33 lakhs of rupees, in the reign of Jehangir (1606-27), and "on its site a lofty mosque was built at the expenditure of a large sum", and, "such a wonderful and seemingly impossible work was successfully accomplished"..

This shows, unmistakably, that:

(1) instead of protecting its subjects, Aurangzeb's state wreaked 'barbarism' upon them, and 'vandalism' upon their shrines which were not only religious buildings, but also wonderful works of art and architecture, and this was done at large expense;
(2) this state forcibly and illegitimately occupied the land of the temple and raised a mosque upon it, in each case; and
(3) all this was done in the name of Islam.

Instead of being an agency of governance, Aurangzeb's state acted as an instrument of 'barbarism' and 'vandalism', and there cannot be any justification, whatsoever, of the iconoclasm unleashed by Aurangzeb upon his own people and within his own kingdom. He was collecting *kharaj* (land-revenue) and *'jaziyah'* (poll-tax) from his non-believing subjects, viz. the *zimmis,* and, as such, it was his sacred obligation to protect their life, property, freedom and religion. He broke the basic laws of Islamic civilization, stipulated in such verses of the Quran as II.256 (*HQ,* 103), CIX .1-6 (*HQ,* 1800) and IX.29 (*HQ,* 447), cited above, ruthlessly. The 'barbarism' and 'vardaism' perpetrated by his state upon its own subjects who were *'zimmis'* was not prescribed by Islam and was not representative of Islamic Civilization. This makes a distinction between the Prophet's Islam and Aurangzeb' s Islam, as broadly as is the distinction between 'Civilization' and 'Barbarism'

The basic Question: The Land of Mosque and the Principle of Legitimacy, *(Haqq)*

It must be reiterated that the rise of Islam, in 7th century Arabia, denoted a step from the primitive *jahiliyah* (ignorance) period into the direction of civilization, with a view to establish the Rule of Law. The Qur-an, the word of God, in fact, codified these laws social, religious and others. *Hadiths* or Traditions or saying of the Prophet and his companions supplement this code in various matters and are second in authority only to the Quran. The two together constitute *shari'ah'* or *shari'at.*

One *Hadith* records that after the Prophet emigrated from Mecca to Madina in 622 A.D., he decided to build there a *masjid* (the place where *'sajdah'* or *'sijdah'* = prostration to God is done; mosque) or place of worship of his religion. A vacant land was found suitable for this purpose. It was owned by two orphans Sahal and Suhayl, who offered it to the Prophet *gratis.* But he refused to accept the land for the purpose of building a mosque on it, without paying its price, or compensation for it and, consequently, a sum of ten *dinars* was paid to them and the Prophet's Mosque at al madinah, *viz* – the Masjidu' n-Nabi was built on this lawfully and legitimately acquired land.

This established, once and for all, the Principle of Legitimacy *(Haqq)* in Islam, that land for a mosque cannot be acquired forcibly, i.e., by barbarous means, but only in accordance with the Rule of Law, i.e., by paying due price or compensation to the owner. This has also been specifically, laid down in the Quran:

> 'Never stand thou forth therein,
> there is a mosque whose foundation
> was laid from the first day
> on piety; it is more worthy
> Of thy standing forth (for prayer)
> therein. In it are men who
> Love to be purified; and
> God Loveth those who make themselves pure'
> (IX.1O8) , *HQ,* 473).

It warns the believers not to go for prayer to any other mosque (referred to in the preceding verse), but to his own mosque whose, foundation was laid from the first day on piety' which means, incontrovertibly, the mosque whose land was legitimately acquired by payment of the price or compensation; the 'foundation' and the first day denote land; and 'piety' denotes *'haqq'* or legitimacy. This dictum ordained that a mosque of Islam must be built only on a legitimately acquired land and it is unlawful in Islam to build a mosque on a land which has been forcibly and wrongfully acquired, by barbarous means, and if a mosque is built on such a land, prayer (*namaz*) offered therein is not valid and is not accepted by God. There are several other *hadiths* which support this law.

The legitimacy of the land is also essential for the legitimacy of '*vaqf*' which is a dedication or endowment of property, of a perpetual nature, made for charitable uses and in the service of God, and is specifically applicable to 'mosque'. The basic condition of a '*vaqf*' is that the property to be endowed, i.e. the land and the building together, must have been legitimately owned by the maker of the 'vaqf or by the community. There cannot be a '*vaqf*' of a property which has been forcibly acquired by plunder or demolition of an existing structure and, as such, it cannot be drafted in the service of 'Allah'.'Piety' (*haqq*) of the Quran IX. 108 means legitimacy which was, broadly, the principle on which Islamic civilization was based. It had nothing to do with the 'barbarism' preached by the Mullas and practiced by the iconoclasts in the name of '*jihad*'.

It is noteworthy that this principle guided all legitimate, sovereign and civilized states of Islam through the ages. We have illustrative examples from the Great Mughals of India. Lahauri, court historian of Shah Jehan (reign, 1628-58) recorded in his history, the *Badshah-Namah,* that when the Jami' Masjid of Agra (built 1644-48) was proposed to be built, facing the Delhi-Gate of Agra Fort, it was reported to the King that there were some houses of the people of the city on this land. He ordered that these houses may be purchased by paying 10 or 15 times of the (market) value to their owners. Satisfactory compensation paid and the land, was, thus, legitimately acquired:

('ki ba-sarkar aqdas t' alluq dasht khanah chand-i-az saknah
shahr ki zamin an dakhil masjid shud shoo barkhi ra ba-bahai
dah panjdah kharidand- va lakhti ra munazil evaz dadah
malikah an-ra khursand gardanidan'[8].

This shows that the Principle of Legitimacy (*Haqq*) was followed by the Muslim states right since the Prophet built the first mosque at Madina and prescribed that a mosque could be built and *drafted* for prayer (*namaz*) only on lawfully acquired land, and this was the only way a Muslim state could act within its own territory. Otherwise, it was illegitimate, and prayer offered therein was not legal and valid. Unfortunately, owing to the misinterpretations of the fanatical mullas who did not distinguish between '*shari' at*' (religion) and '*siyasat*' (politics), and freely mixed one with the other, Islam has been largely misrepresented as an iconoclastic religion, and it is, in fact, this way that the non-believing world looks at it. The basic tenets of religious tolerance and peaceful co-existence of Islamic civilization, as laid down in the Quran (II.256, CIX. I-6, IX.29 etc, as cited above) have been buried under a plethora of later interpretations of the mullas (theologians).

Medieval 'iconoclasm' has now assumed the form of 'terrorism', and the most unfortunate aspect of it is that, in either case, it is unjustly associated with Islam which did not permit the former in medieval times, nor the latter today. It is true that law and faith are inseparable in Islam, and Islamic polity is, essentially, a theocracy. But it is a theocracy within the ambit of CIVILIZATION, and it is not a barbarous phenomenon of the mullas' version. To live with the rest of the humanity, with peace and amity, Islam will have to disassociate itself from those barbarous accretions which the plunderers, despots and tyrants imposed upon it in the later ages, with the connivance of the ever-indulgent mullas, and return to the original purity, simplicity and good intentions of the socio-religious reformatory mission of the Prophet's Islam.

This is, essentially, a civilizational conflict, and it cannot be resolved in pieces: an Ayodhya today, a Kashi tomorrow, a Mathura day-after-tomorrow, and a Dhar after that, and so on and so forth, *ad-infinitum.* Let us face the whole question, once and for all: whether demolition of a temple and forcible acquisition of its land for construction of a mosque thereupon, is an act of Islamic Civilization, and is prescribed by the *'shari'at'*; or, it is an act of barbarism., not approved by Islam. Let there be a categorical answer: it is an act of Islamic Civilization and we approve; or, it is not an act of Islamic Civilization and we disapprove.

In the former case, they would be preaching 'barbarism' which has absolutely no place in the modern world. 'Barbarism' breeds barbarism in reaction, and those who practice it, cannot expect anything else in return. As discussed above, Islam never meant to propagate barbarism. It was born as a civilization and, without the perverted interpretations imposed upon it, during the medieval ages, it can be happily metamorphosed into a 21st century modern, civilized phenomenon. There is no scope, whatsoever, for iconoclasm or terrorism *vis-a-vis* other civilizations of the world, and if the humanity, as a single entity, has to survive, barbarism will have to be buried, and its medieval LEGACY refuted.

References

1. Abdullah Yusuf Ali, *The Holy Quran*, 3. volumes, p.xx+1-1849, 1937-38, abbreviated *HQ* hereinafter
2. *Sahihu'l-Muslim* tr. of Al-Kami'us-Sahih of Imam Muslim by A. H. Siddiqui, 4-vols. Lahore, 1987, abb. *Muslim* hereinafter
3. The *Quran* and *Hadith* together constitute *'shari'ah'* or *'shari'at'*
4. *Ma'asir-i-Alamgiri* of Saqi Must'ad Khan Tr. by Jadunath Sarkar, Calcutta, 1947 aab. *MA* hereinafter
5. *Ibid.*, pp 53-55, 60, 106, 108-109, 115-120 etc
6. *Ibid.*, p 50
7. *Ibid.*, p 60
8. Abdul Hamid Lahauri *Badshah Namah* 1.11.252

Rulers, Urban Milieu and Temple Patronage: Shifting Contours in Rajasthan, (c.A.D.700-1000)

Shanta Sharma*

The numerous extant temple remains are a living testimony to the large-scale temple construction undertaken in c. A.D. 700-1000 Rajasthan.[1] The Osia temple complex, consisting of as many as eleven temples dedicated to different deities. Śiva, Sūrya, Harihara, Saciyāmātā, Piplāmātā, and Mahāvīra,[2] gives evidence of temple building by the followers of the various brahmanical sects as well as the Jaina devotees. A district wise survey of temples on the basis of available epigraphic and monumental evidence[3] reveals their wide distribution all over Rajasthan. Temple building acquired new dimensions with the evolution of the Mahā-Māru and Mahā-Gurjara styles of architecture,[4] the attractive pañchāyatana form,[5] and stylistic variety of temple sculptures.[6]

The present study perceives the operation of major transitional historical processes of political, economic and religious interactions in the shaping of contemporary temple patronage. In the political context, it investigates and identifies the correlation between the shifting contours of patronage and the grants made by the emergent ruling lineages of Rajasthan that supplanted the erstwhile tribal polity. Later famed as the Rajputs, these lineages included the Cāhamānas of Śakambhari, the Guhilas of Mewar, the Rāṣṭrakūṭas of Hathundi, Pratihāras of Rajor and the Imperial Pratihāras.[7] In the economic context, it explores the links of temple patronage with the urban milieu, taking due note of the temple donations emanating from merchants, artisans and exchange centres. These are historically significant as considerable evidence of urban development characterized by commercial activity, monetary exchange, craft specialisation, social mobility, artistic and architectural vitality, secular orientation and social administration etc. has emerged from various settlements in Rajasthan from seventh century onwards.[8]

A twofold focus is adopted in the present article to elaborate and elucidate the outlined perspective. Firstly, an in-depth study of epigraphic evidence is made to gain a concrete idea of the patrons, temple maintenance provisions made by the builders as well as the extent and nature of temple endowments and their management. Secondly, an analytical assessment is presented to reveal the nature of transformation in temple patronage and resources due to change in the character of the donors and endowments over the centuries under consideration. Further, to complete the historical analysis, the reasons why patronage in Rajasthan did not lead to a Chola type temple

*Reader, History Dept., Dayal Singh College, Delhi University, New Delhi

economy are considered and a brief scrutiny of subsequent political developments is undertaken to assess the lasting worth of the grants.

Though many temples can be identified as eighth century edifices, not many inscriptions of the period are available(table:1). The A.D. 738-39 Kanaswa (Kota district) inscription records construction of a temple by the brahmana prince Śivagaṇa and his grant of two villages to the temple.[9] The fragmentary inscription from Śankaraghaṭṭā dated A.D. 770 records the construction of a high structure, probably a temple, by the king Mānabhaṅga.[10] Document no. VII of the Kaman (Bharatpur district) set of inscriptions, dated A.D. 786, records the donation of two enclosures conferred by a worker in conch-shells (*śaṁkhika*) to an existing temple.[11] The fragmentary A.D. 788 Tasai inscription, which records the building of a temple by a person named Raṇyāditya, also mentions certain objects, which were apparently granted in favour of the deity. These include 2 *palas* of oil for the lamp, 2 palas of incense called *guggula*, 40 garlands and 8 *māṣakas* of saffron, which were supplied every day.[12] The A.D. 790 Kota inscription records the construction of a Buddhist temple by the *sāmanta* Devadatta.[13]

Two other inscriptions assigned to the eighth century on paleographic grounds are from Kalyanpur and Kaman. The Kaman inscription records the construction of a temple by Vaccika wife of Durgadaman.[14] The fragmentary Kalyanpur inscription of the time of kadachi apparently a ruling chief, records the construction of a temple by his wife Vonna. The lady made a grant of 40 dramma coins (per month or year) for the carrying out of repairs to the breaks and damages in the said temple, for the burning of *guggula* before the deity worshipped therein and for the sweeping of the floor and compound of the temple.[15]

Out of the seven inscriptions recording temple patronage, only four contain donations. Among these, the Kanaswa grant alone proceeds directly from a ruler. The identity of the donor of the Tasai donation is not known. The Kaman donation of two enclosures (*avaris*) by a *śāṁkhika* indicates the acquisition of immovable property and acceptance of gifts from the ritually lower order of artisans to the temple. Of the two c. 8th century inscriptions at Kaman and Kalyanpur recording patronage by women, the latter provides evidence of a cash donation. Rulers and their relatives, artisans, specialised commodities such as oil and saffron as well as coined money figure in temple patronage. But the conferred donations are meagre when compared to the substantial grants made in later times and there is no record of the tapping of urban resources such as commercial cesses for the purpose.

In the ninth century, Kāmyakeśvara at Kaman emerges as a major beneficiary of religious endowments(table:2). An A.D. 826 document records the gift of three plough-measures of land by a person named Untaṭa. In A.D. 835 a gift of two plots of land was made by a person whose name is now missing. Three successive documents from A.D. 835, A.D. 838 and A.D. 839 record that the guilds of potters, gardeners and artisans living in Kāmyaka, in considera-

Table I: Grants in the 8th century

Date	Place	Patron	Nature of Patronage	
			Built temple	Gave donation
A.D. 738-39	Kanaswa	Prince	Built temple	2 villages
A.D. 770	śaṅkaraghaṭṭā	King	Built temple	-----------
A.D. 786	Kaman	Conch-shell worker	------------	2 enclosures
A.D. 788	Tasai	Raṇyāditya	Built temple	Oil, incense, saffron
A.D. 790	Kota	Sāmanta	Built temple	--------------
c. 8th cent.	Kaman	Vaccikā	Built temple	--------------
c. 8th cent.	Kalyanpur	Voṇṇā	Built temple	Coins

tion of an amount paid in advance to each one of them, stipulated to pay respectively a permanent cess of one *pana* (coin) per wheel every month, the permanent supply of sixty garlands and one' *dramma* (coin) perartisan. An eighth century document records certain donations by a merchant, the nature of which is not clear.[16] The Kāmyakeśvara temple thus was a recipient of grants of cash, land and kind.

Many temples were built in the ninth century. The Khandela inscription of A.D. 807 records the building of a temple by Ādityanāga, grandson of Durgavardhana, a vaṇik[17]. In A.D. 815, the Buckala inscription records construction of a temple by a queen Jayāvalī, whose husband was most probably a chieftain subordinate to Nāgabhaṭa II.[18] The Sakrai inscription, A.D. 822, records the construction of an excellent pavilion of gods (maṇḍapa) by an association consisting of eleven members, including *śreṣṭhins* and *vaṇiks.*[19] The Dholpur inscription, A.D. 842, records the building of a temple by Candamahasena, a ruler of the Dholpur branch of Cāhamānas.[20] In A.D. 861, the Mandor Pratihāra ruler Kakkuka established a Jina temple at Mandor.[21] A separate inscription from Kaman dated A.D. 869 records the construction of a temple by three brothers.[22]

Out of the twelve records, the six containing donations are all from Kaman. There is no record of the builders of the other temples, who include rulers, the wife of a ruling chieftain, *śreṣṭhins* and merchants conferring any accompanying donations. However the role played in temple patronage by the different guilds of potters, gardeners and artisans as well as the monetary investment and grants at Kaman reflect the contribution of the forces of urbanism. Merchants figure as temple patrons at Kaman, Khandela and Sakrai and the rulers at Mandor and Dholpur.

The equation changes in the tenth century with donations of cash, fields, villages and taxes including market levies by rulers, traders and individuals. According to the Kaman document dated A.D. 905, the temple of Kamyakesvara received yet another grant of some *'drammas'.* Earlier given by Sri Bhojadeva to Pramāṇarāsi, and by him to Chāmuṇḍaka, who handed them over to the temple goṣṭhi, the *'drammas'* were utilised by the latter to purchase two enclosures with shops for the temple.[23]

The extensive patronage extended by the Hastikundi (Hathundi) Rāṣtrakūtas to the Jaina temple located at their capital Hathundi is recorded in the inscriptions found at Bijapur. The inscription of the Rāṣtrakūta ruler Mammaṭa, A.D. 939, records that the temple was erected by his predecessor Vidagdha. The

Table 2: Grants in the 9th century

Date	Place	Patron	Nature of Patronage	
			Built Temple	Gave Donation
A.D. 826	Kaman	Untaṭa	-----------	3 plough measures
A.D. 835	Kaman	---------	-----------	2 plots of land
A.D. 835	Kaman	Guild of potters	------------	Monetary grant
A.D. 838	Kaman	Guild of gardeners	-----------	Garlands
A.D. 839	Kaman	Guild of artisans	-----------	Monetary grant
8th cent.	Kaman	Merchant	------------	Not clear
A.D. 807	Khandela	Merchant	Built temple	
A.D. 815	Buchkala	Queen	Built temple	----------
A.D. 822	Sakrai	Śreṣthins	Built pavilion	----------
A.D. 842	Dholpur	Ruler	Built temple	----------
A.D. 861	Mandor	Ruler	Built temple	---------
A.D. 869	Kaman	3 brothers	Built temple	---------

grant made in favour of the temple by Vidagdha in A.D. 916 was renewed by Mammaṭa in A.D. 939. Two-thirds of the proceeds accruing from the collection of various taxes and tolls were assigned to the temple thereby, *viz.* (1) one *rūpaka* coin for each twenty loads carried for sale, (2) one *rūpaka* on each cart filled (whether going from or by the place), (3) one *karṣa* for a ghaḍā at each oil-mill, (4) thirteen *collikās* of betel-leaves by the *bhattas* (5) one *āḍhaka* (=4 seers) of wheat and barley from each *araghaṭṭa,* i.e. well with a water-wheel, (6) one *viṁśopaka* coin from each *bhāra* (=2000 palas), (7) ten *palas* from each *bhāra* of articles, such as cotton, copper, saffron, gum-resin (*pura,* i.e. guggulu), madder and so forth, and (8) one *māṇaka* from each *droṇa* of wheat, mung, barley, salt, and such other objects as can be measured[24]. A subsequent inscription, dated A.D. 997, records that Mammaṭa's successor Dhavala, in conjunction with his son, made the gift of a well.[25]

Gifts of cash as well as kind were thus made to the temple by the Rāṣhtrakūta rulers. The nature of the donations indicates the tapping of resources generated from a major centre of exchange, where a sizable volume of commodities converged These included a variety of agricultural goods, manufactured items and raw material. The evidence of large-scale mercantile activity, levies realised in cash and tolls on movement and sale of commodities indicate the urban spatial context of Hathundi.

Various grants made in favour of different shrines at Ghotarsi at different times are recorded in the Partabgarh inscription. According to the grant dated A.D. 946, Mahendrapala II, the Imperial Pratihāra ruler, on the request of a certain Dhana-śūra, bestowed a village situated in the vicinity of Ghoṇṭa-varṣikā (modern Ghotrasi) upon the goddess Vaṭa-yakṣiṇi-devī. The village was granted with the customary contributions in kind *(bhāgabhogakara)* and cash *(hiraṇya)* due to the ruler. An accompanying undated grant records that the goddess also received a permanent endowment from the trading community. This comprised of one *palikā* (of oil) per oil-mill, five bundles of foliage, hundred garlands of four strings, together with two *pala* of saffron and one *pala* of betel-nuts from the trading community in the month of *chaitra.*[26]

Another grant at Partabgarh, which is undated, records that Mādhava, the governor of Ujjain (under Mahendrapāla) at the request of the *mahāsāmanta* Indrarāja, son of Durlabharāja of, the Cāhamāna family (of the Partabgarh branch), granted a village to the temple of Indraditya- deva at Ghoṇṭa-varṣika.The village was granted along with the ruler's right to revenue payment in cash and kind *(bhāga, bhoga, kara, hiraṇya, skandhaka)* apparently a cess at a certain rate per load and mārgaṇaka (benevolences of a general character levied upon the villages). Evidently the Cāhamāna ruler Indrarāja built the temple that was named after him and then applied to his overlord for a grant for its upkeep. A further endowment of a field and five matting screens for the erection of a flower porch by Mādhava to the temple is recorded thereafter.[27] The same temple, described as Indrarājāditya-deva of Ghoṇṭa-varṣi received the bestowal of a field from Bhartṛpaṭṭa, son of Khommāṇa, evidently the Guhila ruler of Mewar, in A.D. 942.[28] There is also the grant of a field in favour of Indrāditya-deva by Deva-rāja, son of Chamuṇḍa-rāja.[29]

Partabgarh also has an undated grant of Indrarāja, evidently the scion of the Cāhamāna family noted earlier, of a field in favour of Trailokyamohanadeva in the grounds of Indrāditya-deva. There is also a record of the gift of two fields, in each of which ten *māṇīs* of seed could be sown, from persons not mentioned and in favour of deities not specified.[30] Thus we have gifts of fields, villages, cash and kind made to different temples by individuals, members of the trading community, rulers and an official on the behalf of the ruler.

The mention of *skandhaka,* a tax levied on movement of goods, and revenue payments in cash by villagers indicate making over of profits from ongoing exchange of commodities and a monetary economy. The corporate religious donations made by the traders endowments from, oil-mills underline the substantial contribution made by non-agricultural sections.

The Āhar-Sāranesvara temple, A.D. 953, records the construction of a Viṣṇu temple during the reign of Allaṭa, the Guhila ruler of Mewar. Donations for it were specifically fixed by Allaṭa who specifically laid down that they should not be refused by the merchants of Karṇāṭa, Madhyadeśa, Lāṭa and Ṭakka, or by any others who came there. These included one *dramma* to be taken on (the sale of) an elephant, two *rūpakas* on a horse, one-fortieth of a *dramma* on a horned animal, one *tula* from a lāṭa and one ādhaka from a haṭṭa. On the eleventh day of the bright fortnight of a month, one *ghaṭikā-pala* (of milk) was donated from every saucepan (of confectioners), one *peṭaka* from the gamblers, one *pala* of oil from every oil mill, one *rūpaka* from the randhanī at the end of a month, and one *catuhas* (four-stringed garland) from the flower-sellers everyday.[31]

The Guhila ruler thus made over the profits from a major centre of exchange. These included (a) taxes levied on inter-regional traders from the faraway region of Karnataka, as well as Gujarat, Punjab and mid-India, (b) sales tax realised from the traders of long distance high value commodities like horses and elephants and (c) agricultural produce sold at the market place *(haṭṭa)*.

The A.D. 955 Bayana inscription of queen Citralekhā, who was a descendant of the Śūrasena family and subordinate to Mahipāla, records that she caused a temple to be built, with a crest-jewel shaped as a golden egg and adorned with flags. She donated two villages as well as fields to the deity. She also arranged that three *drammas* were given every day by the customs house *(maṇḍapikā)* at Śrīpathā and also another three by the customs house at Vusāvata. A gift of one *dramma* per horse was also fixed, either collected on every horse sold or on every horse-load of merchandise.[32]

The temple donations made by the Bayana ruler thus included revenue from a regular centre of exchange, through which considerable commercial traffic passed. The daily cash collections, the setting up of more than one mandapika and reference to horses/horse loads among items of merchandise reveal that transit of goods formed a major commercial activity and the spatial context was urban.

In A.D. 960, as recorded by the Rajor inscription, Mathanadeva, evidently a ruler subordinate to the imperial Pratihāra ruler Vijayapāla, granted the village of Vyāghrapāṭaka to a temple established by him. It was granted along with various dues, including the shares of all sorts of grain, the cess from the threshing floor (*khala-bhikṣā*), *prasthaka* (a cess on each prastha measure of liquids or on each *prastha* over and above the usual grain-share) and *skandhaka*.[33] There were also certain additional taxes or tolls, the proceeds of which were to be made over to the same temple along with the god Vinayak (whose image or shrine was) set up nearby. These included three *viṁśopakas*, as customary in the market (*haṭṭa*), on every sack (of agricultural produce) brought for sale to the market, two palikas from every ghataka-kupaka of clarified butter and oil, two *viṁśopakas* per mensem for every shop, and fifty leaves from every collikā (of leaves) brought from outside the town.[34]

Evidently the ruler supplemented the village grant with various taxes arising from an urban context. Among these proceeds issuing from activities connected with the *haṭṭa* or market place, recorded in the inscription in a portion separate from the land grant, were (a) cash levies on agricultural produce and shops (b) imposts in kind raised from dealers in butter and oil and (c) levy in kind imposed on the import of leaves. The mention of *skandhaka* among the village dues gives indication of the movement of goods in the village as well.

The Jagat inscription of A.D. 960 recording the construction of a temple by a person named Samvapura, son of Valluka, does not mention any grant.[35] The Ekalingajī inscription of the time of Guhila king Naravāhana, A.D. 971, records that certain Pasupata sages erected a temple and dedicated it to Lakulisa.[36] No mention is made of any grant.

The temple of Harshanātha, Sikar district,

received the patronage of the Śākambharī branch of Cāhamānas. It appears to have been originally built by Gūvaka I and renovated by the sage Allaṭa in A.D. 956.[37] The Harṣa inscription of the time of Vigraharāja II records the various endowments to the temple received up to A.D. 973. The ruler Simharāja granted four villages; his brother Vatsarāja gifted one village; the ruler Vigraharāja, the son of Siṁharāja, granted two villages; Siṁharāja's other two sons Chandrarāja and Govindarāja gifted two hamlets. Dhandhuka, an official of Siṁharāja's, and a certain Jayanīraja also granted a village each. Likewise, for the benefit of the temple, one *viṁśopaka* on every *kūṭaka* of salt at Śākambharī was assigned by the Bhammaha guild, and one *dramma* on every horse by the horse-dealers. Various pious people also gave fields in five different villages, besides a big plough of land. Mention is also made of Siṁharāja having set a golden dome on the temple.[38] An appraisal of the donors to the temple reveals that the temple stood to gain from cash grants from ongoing organised mercantile activity in addition to the land endowments by the rulers and the people. Dealers in salt as well as horses were participants in temple patronage.

The Atpur (Ahar) inscription, A.D. 977, records the erection of a temple in the reign of Śaktikumāra.[39] Though it gives various details of his genealogy, it does not mention any donation. But we have another inscription at Ahar, which records that the previously existing practice of offering fourteen *drammas* each year to another deity was continued during the reign of Śaktikumāra.[40]

The Mandakila Tal inscription, A.D. 987, records the building of a temple by a śreṣṭhin named Nandana at Nagar. Equipped with a storeroom and a well in front, the temple was durable, embellished with metal (plating) and provided with nine entrance-doors. It was also whitewashed, with massive pillars and beautiful with stone-slabs properly fixed. There is mention of Nandana having made endowments for proper worship of the installed deities and then breathed his last, but no details of the endowments are given. Reference is made to his grandfather Nārāyana having built lofty temples as also the building of a temple by Nārāyana's grandfather, Nāgahari.[41] The epigraph thus provides ample evidence of temple patronage by the prosperous *śreṣṭhins* of Nagar.

It is apparent from table no.3 that the temple donations substantially increase during the tenth century. An idea of the considerable pecuniary resources

Table 3: Grants in the 10th century

Date	Place	Patron	Nature of Patronage: Built temple	Nature of Patronage: Gave patronage
A.D. 905	Kaman	Āchārya	--------------	Monetary grant
A.D. 916	Hathundi	Ṛāṣṭrakūṭa ruler Vidagdha	Built temple	Levies from centre of exchange, monetary grant
A.D. 939	Hathundi	Ṛāṣṭrakūṭa ruler Maṁmaṭa	--------------	Levies from centre of ex change, monetary grant
A.D. 942	Partabgarh	Guhila ruler Bhartṛpaṭṭa	--------------	Field
A.D. 946	Partabgarh	Pratihāra ruler Mahendrapāla II	--------------	Village with dues in cash and kind
A.D. 946	Partabgarh	Trading community	-------------	Industrial, commercial items

c.10th cent.	Partabgarh	Pratihāra governor at request of subordinate Cāhamāna ruler Indrarāja	Temple built by Indraraja	Village with dues in cash and kind
c.10th cent.	Partabgarh	Pratihāra governor	-------------	Field and 5 matting screens
c.10th cent.	Partabgarh	Cāhamāna ruler Indrāraja	------------	Field
c.10th cent.	Partabgarh	Various individuals	------------	5 fields
A.D. 953	Āhār	Guhila ruler Allata	------------	Cash levies on traders and sale of commodities
A.D. 955	Bayana	Śurasena ruler	Built temple	2 villages and custom dues in cash
A.D. 960	Rajor	Rajor pratihara ruler	Built temple	Village with various dues, market levies
A.D. 960	Jagat	Individual	Built temple	------------
A.D. 971	Ekalingi	Pāśupata sages	Built temple	------------
A.D. 973	Harṣa	Various Cahamana rulers of Śākambharī	Built temple	7 villages, 2 hamlets
A.D. 973	Harsha	Guilds of horse dealers and salt dealers	-------------	Monetary grant
A.D. 977	Āhār	Guhila ruler Śaktikumāra	Built temple	------------
c.10th cent.	Āhār	Guhila ruler Śaktikumāra and predecessor	------------	Monetary grant
A.D. 987	Mandakila Tal	Line of merchants	Built temple	Endowment

and landed property at the disposal of these temples can be seen from the following tabulation:-

Temple site	Resources in landed property, cash and kind
Āhār Sāraneśhvara	tolls and taxes yielding cash and kind
Āhār Sāraneśhvara	regular annual cash donation
Bayana	two villages, tolls from customs house
Harṣa	nine villages, two hamlets, monetary grant
Hathundi	taxes yielding cash and kind
Kaman (A.D. 786-905)	three plough measures of land, two plots of land and, cash returns from guilds, rent from guilds, rent from two enclosures with shops
Partabgarh complex	two villages, six fields, endowment from trading community yielding cash as well as kind
Rajor	village and various levies from market

No donations made to the temples at Osia, Jagat, Ekalingaji, Catsu, Atpur and Nagar are recorded.

The accumulation of temple resources through donations from different sources over the years led to an attempt at systematic recording of the grants to various temples in the tenth century. The Kaman set of inscriptions brought together eight grants, the dates of which range from A.D. 786 to A.D. 905.[42] The Partabgarh grants of Mahendrapāla II, Bhartṛpaṭṭa, Indrarāja and various individuals proffered to three temples existing in close proximity and evidently under the same management were also collated in a single grant.[43] The Harsha grant carefully recorded not only the grants made by the ruling king, his brothers and his predecessors but various other individual grants as well.[44] The Bijapur inscription brought together two independent records pertaining to the endowments made by the earlier ruler Vidaghda and the reigning king.[45]

The vast increase in temple wealth is partly due to the fact that in contrast to the eighth and ninth centuries, when rulers rarely gave grants for the maintenance of temples, in the tenth century various rulers assigned grants to temples, either previously existing or established by them or their predecessors. In the first category falls the Imperial Pratihāra ruler Mahendrapāla II who assigned two villages to different temples, one directly and another through his governor. The first was assigned at the request of an individual whose status is not mentioned and another at the request of the builder of the temple, a subordinate Cāhamāna ruler.[46] This is significant as there is little epigraphic evidence of the patronage of temples by the Imperial Pratiharas.[47] Among the Guhilas of Mewar, a field is granted by Bhartṛpaṭṭa II, son of Khommāṇa, to a temple established by a Cāhamāna rulers of Śākambharī.[48] Allaṭa granted various tolls and taxes to a temple set up by various dignitaries.[49] Śaktikumāra continued an earlier established cash grant to a temple on the request of Mattaṭa, his *akṣapaṭalādhipati*.[50] In the second category, the maximum number of grants were made by the Cāhamāna rulers of Śākaṁbharī. Village grants were made by Siṁharāja and his brother to a temple built by their predecessor Gūvaka I, three generations earlier. Subsequently it received grants from Siṁharāja's successor Vigraharāja II and his brothers as well.[51] The rulers of Bayana[52] and Rajor[53],evidently subordinate to the Pratihāra rulers, made over not only grants of villages but taxes and tolls to the temples they established. The Rāṣṭrakūtas of Hathundi granted various levies.[54]

Another crucial variable of the tenth century temple assets was the urban milieu, reflected in the assignment of market levies to temples. This was either in the form of voluntary donations by traders as at Partabgarh[55] and Harsanatha[56] or the assignment of commercial cesses as at Rajor[57], Ahar[58], Bayana[59] and Hathundi.[60] Assignment of taxes collected on the sale of different commodities, *viz.* agricultural commodities at Rajor, animals at Ahar Saranesvara, horses or horse-loads of merchandise at Bayana, and loads carried for sale at Hathundi indicates the channeling of benefits derived from an urban context. The same is reflected in the endowments made by the Partabgarh trading community as well as the Bhammaha guild and the horse-dealers at Harṣanātha.[61] The ongoing trade in varied commodities constituted an important source of temple resources. Donations raised from various commercial and industrial items, *viz.*, cotton, copper, saffron, gum-resin, madder, wheat, mung, barley, salt, betel-leaves at Hathund, foliage, saffron, and betel-nuts at Partapgarh, salt and horses at Harṣa and the oil-mills at Hathundl and Ahar are recorded in epigraphs. Levies on the movement of agricultural products and the varied agricultural crops, essential elements of urban consumption, were also made over.[62] There is also evidence of donations derived from the use of a relatively advanced hydraulic technology, the araghaṭṭa or water-wheel at Partapgarh[63] and Hathundi.[64]

Assignation of part of the proceeds from two *mandapikas*, generally taken to signify a customhouse, at Bayana[65], further indicate the tapping of available market resources. Recurrent cash grants bestowed on the temples at Ahar Sāraneśvara, Bayana, Harṣa, Hathundi, Partapgarh, and Rajor[66], via assignment of various cesses are indicative of the advantage taken of the prevalent money economy. At

Ahar[67] and earlier at Kaman[68], provision was made for the cash to be delivered at regular intervals. At Kaman the temple took full advantage of the prevalent market economy by investing in guilds as well as purchasing shops and renting them out.[69]

Generous donations made by the general populace continued to be an important factor in the increase of temple wealth. The credit for the renovation of the Harsa temple with the addition of well-constructed halls is given to the sage Allaṭa who received the wealth from pious people. The temple also received liberal grants from individuals.[70] Similarly the credit for the renovation of the temple at Hathundi also does not belong to the ruler, but to certain individuals.[71]

The temples of Rajasthan during this period did not develop a vast Chola scale economy, where the temples were so well endowed that they gave loans to village assemblies from the temple treasury and kept a large assemblage of servants.[72] Nor did they hold cows and sheep that they assigned to shepherds. The factors inhibiting such a parallel development in Rajasthan are not far to seek. A scrutiny of the purpose of the earlier grants, where it is stated, indicates that they were allocated for a comparatively limited purpose. The Kanaswa grant was for provision of incense, perfumes and lights.[73] The eighth century Kalyanpur grant was for repairs to breaks and damages.[74] According to the Kaman document III, the rent accrued was to be utilized for meeting the expenses of whitewashing, vermilion and lights.[75] The Partabgarh grant of Madhava was made for repairs and maintenance of daily service.[76] These grants were of limited extent and could not support a Chola style temple establishment.

A significant departure was made in the Harṣa grant of Siṁharāja, which in addition to bathing, worshipping and anointing (the god), oblations, incense and lamps also provided for the celebration of processions on festive days.[77] The Rajor grant was made not only for the, defraying the expenses of bathing (the god) three times a day, of unguents, flowers, incense, *naivedya* offerings, lights and oil, of applying white-wash and lead, of repairing what may become damaged or broken but also for public shows, putting on the sacred thread, and paying labourers, gardeners etc.[78] In the Bayana grant mention is made of (girls) with armlets, shining necklaces, jeweled anklets, bracelets and girdles of gold, appearing like wishing-creepers, indicating the presence of dancing girls. A show given by these ladies was arranged by the queen.[79] Thus, while the earlier grants only made provision for the needs of daily worship, the later grants provided for processions of the deity and public shows, with evidently the additional provision of dancing girls at Bayana. However the intention remained the same as earlier, *viz.* the extension of temple activities intimately associated with the worship of the deity.

A study of the activities at the Harsa temple, which received an unparalleled number of grants after a long period of initial neglect subsequent to the building of a temple by a Cāhamāna ruler, gives valuable insight into the working of the temples. The dedicated Śaiva ascetics, who led a life of supreme self-abnegation[80], utilized the wealth placed at their disposal solely for the renovation of the temple. According to the Harṣa inscription the temple presented a glorious sight, lovely in consequence of the statues of Vikaṭa and the sons of Pāṇḍu set up in a row, an excellent doorway and a well-carved bull. Further additions to the temple renovated in A.D. 956 were made sometime between A.D. 970 to A.D. 973. These included the execution of an excellent well, a beautiful garden for worship with flowers and a cistern for providing water to cattle. A court paved with smooth stones, level and pleasant for walking was also built.[81] Thus the effort was towards a substantial expansion of temple facilities for devotees and beautification rather than ministering to the comforts of temple priests. Naturally, given this orientation the recruitment of countless temple staff could not be envisaged.

Further, how substantial these resources were and whether they remained at the disposal of these temples for long is open to question. There was no aura of inviolability surrounding temple donations, making them sacrosanct, once bestowed. Market levies made over by a particular ruler, notwithstanding the customary decree that they should last as long as the moon, could certainly be rescinded by a successor. This explains why after the elapse of merely twenty-three years the grant of the ruler Vidagdha had to be renewed by his successor Maṁmaṭa.[82] The previously existing cash grant to a temple was renewed by the ruler Śaktikumāra only at the express request of his official Mattaṭa.[83] This would make the hold of temples over donations rather tenuous. Kaman was an exception, where assets were successfully accumulated over a period of hundred years.[84] But then, the temple was not dependent on royal patronage. No village or commercial cesses were donated to it. Donations were purely voluntary and judiciously invested in an urban economy.[85]

In the case of Allaṭa's Āhār Sāraneśvara grant[86], it is difficult to assess the temple wealth, as there are no details regarding the volume of goods passing through and the number of oil-mills, or confectioners etc. The Hathundi inscription of Dhavala, A.D. 997, records the destruction of Ahar by Munja Paramara.[87] The defeated ruler is identified as the Guhila ruler Śaktikumāra[88], whose successor again was slain in battle by the contemporary Cāhamāna ruler[89] thereafter is questionable, especially since they were grants of cash, tolls and taxes made by rulers. Similar grants made by the Rastrakutas of Hathundi must also have been discontinued with their decline soon after.

The Partapgarh grants made by the Imperial Pratihāras also could not have lasted long as their power was fast on the wane. Nothing is known of the successors of Indrarāja, the Cāhamāna ruler of Partapgarh and Mathanadeva, the ruler of Rajor (near Alwar). The impact of the invasions of Mahmud of Ghazni has also to be considered. In A.D. 1009, he attacked Nārāyana which has been identified by Cunningham with Nārāyanpura near Alwar.[90] In A.D. 1018, he defeated the Pratihāra ruler Rājyapāla.

The Harṣanātha temple was the only temple that emerged as a major beneficiary. However the lands endowed to it did not form a contiguous territory but were scattered in different localities *(vishayas),* identified as situated in different parts of the erstwhile Jodhpur and Jaipur states, and the Sikar principality.[91] There is no record of the immediate Cāhamāna successors taking any interest in the temple.[92] The founding of the Nadol (Marwar) branch of the Cāhamānas around the period reveals a considerable diminution in the territory of the Śākambharī Cāhamānas.[93] In the early eleventh century, the Śākambharī branch faced serious reverses with two of their rulers, Vīryarama and Durlabharāja III, losing their life in battle at the hands of the Paramāra and Mātaṅga (probably a Yamini invasion from the north-west) forces respectively.[94] By the twelfth century the kingdom of Sapādalakṣahad ended. It is most unlikely that the grants survived under these circumstances. The patronage received by the Chola temple on the other hand was both generous and sustained.

To conclude, different sections of society belonging to the ritually higher as well as the lower orders, including rulers, women, merchants, artisans and various other individuals extended their patronage to temples in this period. However a distinct change in the nature of patronage is discernable in the tenth century as donations for maintenance became a customary adjunct to the earlier act of temple building. Rulers, who granted villages, fields, tolls and taxes, emerged as significant patrons. Dual benefit of the prevalent urban development accrued to the temple via the assignation of market levies by the rulers as well as voluntary contributions by the merchant community. The resultant expansion of the temple resources was however ephemeral as most of the patron ruling dynasties declined shortly after.

References

1. An extensive survey is presented in M. W. Meister, M.A. Dhaky and Krishna Deva (Ed.) *Encyclopedia of Indian Temple Architecture*, vol. 2, pt.2, *North India: Period of Early Maturity*, c. A.D. 700-900 (henceforth *EITA*), Delhi, 1991
2. Bhandarkar, D.R. 'The Temples of Osia', *Archaeological Survey Annual Report* (henceforth *ASAR*), 1908-9, pp. 100 f
3. Sharma, Shanta Rani 'Urbanism in Rajasthan, (c. A.D. 600-900)', *Journal of Studies on Ancient India* , vol. I, nos. 2-4, 1998, pp. 177 f
4. Dhaky, M.A. 'The Genesis and Development of Maru-Gurjara Temple Architecture *in Studies in India, Temple Architecture*, Ed. Pramod Chandra, Delhi, 1975, pp. 115-16
5. Percy Brown, *Indian Architecture.* 4th ed., Bombay, 1959, p. 135
6. Atherton, C.P. *The Sculpture of Early Medieval Rajasthan*, E. J. Brill, 1997, p. 113
7. The discussion here is restricted to delineation of the shifting contours of patronage. For an analytical and fresh study of the reasons why Shaivism in particular attracted patronage from ruling lineages during the period see the present author's forthcoming article 'Metamorphosis of Shaivism in Rajasthan, c. A.D. 600-1000: The Cult, Sects and Monastic Order to be published soon.
8. Sharma, Shanta Rani 'Urbanism in Rajasthan' (c. A.D. 600-900), *Journal of Studies on Ancient India*, vol. I, nos. 2-4, 1998; idem., *Society and Culture in Rajasthan*, c. A.D. 700-900, Delhi, 1996
9. *Indian Antiquary*, (henceforth *IA*), XIX, pp. 55 f
10. *ASAR*, 1934-35, pp. 56-57
11. *Epigraphia Indica* (henceforth *EI*), XXIV, pp. 329 f
12. *EI*, XXXVI, pp. 49 f
13. *IA*, XIV, pp. 45 f
14. *IA*, X, pp. 34 f
15. *EI*, XXXV, pp. 55 f
16. All these Kaman documents are jointly recorded in *EI*, XXIV, pp. 329 f
17. *EI*, XXXIV, pp. 159 f
18. *EI*, IX, pp. 198 f
19. *EI*, XXVII, pp. 27 f
20. *Zeitschrift der Deutschen Morgenlandischen Gesellschaft*, XL, pp. 38 f., cited D. Sharma, *Early Chauhan Dynasties*, 2nd ed., Delhi, 1975, p. 19
21. *EI*, IX, pp. 277 f
22. *EI*, XXXVI, pp. 52 f
23. *EI*, XXIV, pp. 329 f
24. EI, X, pp. 17 f. *Karsa, adhaka, pala, bhara, manaka* and *drona* denote different weights, cr. P .Niyogi, *Contributions to the Economic History of Northern India*, Calcutta, 1962, chapter IV. U.N. Ghoshal takes *collika* to mean a load-measure, *Contributions to the History of the Hindu Revenue System*, (henceforth *HRS*) 2nd rev. ed., Calcutta, 1972, p. 316
25. *EI*, X, pp. 17 f
26. *EI*, XIV, pp. 176 f. The significance of the fiscal terms *bhaga, bhoga, kara* and *hiranya* has been discussed by several scholars cf. U.N. Ghoshal, *HRS*, pp. 39,45-47, 319; R.S. Tripathi, *History of Kannauj*, Benares, 1937, p. 348; L.Gopal, *Economic History of Northern India*, 2nd rev. ed., Delhi, 1989, pp. 32-33. Ghoshal, on the basis of Arthashastra evidence, established that *bhaga* represented the usual grain-share of the king and *bhoga* the periodical supplies of fruits, firewood, flowers and the like, which the villagers had to furnish to the king. He suggested that *kara* was a general property-tax, levied periodically, *HRS*, pp. 45-47. He identifies the compound *bhagabhogakara* as the usual grain-share of the king, called *bhaga* in the Arthashastra, *Ibid.*, p. 281. L.Gopal also holds that the expression *bhagabhogakara* was often used to refer in a general way to revenue paid in kind, *op.cit.*, p. 33
27. *Ibid.* The explanation of the terms *skandhaka* and *marganaka* has been taken from U.N. Ghoshal, *HRS* pp. 317-8. For further discussion on these terms see D. Sharma, *Rajasthan through the Ages* (henceforth *RTA*), Bikaner, 1966, pp. 327-8
28. *Ibid.*
29. *Ibid.*

30. *Ibid., Mani* is a measure of seed, cr. P. Niyogi, *op.cit.* , pp. 90-113

31. *IA*, LVIII, pp. 161 f. The editor of the inscription, R.R Haldar gives an explanation for many of the terms used. According to him, *tula* stands for the measure of grain which was held in balance in weighing once and *lata* is the division of crops between a peasant and the state. The *haṭṭa* is a market and *ghaṭika pala* is a ladle with a small jar attached to its end. *Petaka* probably means the amount of money won by a gambler at one venture. *Randhani* is taken to refer to a feast

32. *EI*, XXII, pp .120 f

33. *EI*, III, pp. 263 f

34. *Ghaṭaka-kūpaka* is evidently a measure of capacity and *collikā* is evidently a load-measure, U.N. Ghoshal, *HRS*, p. 318. *Palika* is a weight denomination for liquids. For references in other contemporary inscriptions see P. Niyogi, *op. cit.*, p.l09

35. Agrawal, RC. 'Ūnavāsa kā Aggyāt Durḡa Mandir', *Varadā*, VII, iv, pp. 14 --15

36. Bhandarkar, D.R. *JBBRAS*, XXII, pp. 166 f

37. Bhandarkar, D.R *IA*, XLII, pp. 57 f

38. *EI*, II, pp. 116; *IA* XLII, pp.57 f

39. *IA*, XXXIX, pp.186 f

40. Ojha, G.H. *Udaipur Rajya Ka Itihas*, Ajmer, 1985, p. 130

41. *EI*, XXXIV, pp. 77 f

42. *EI*, XXIV, pp. 329 f

43. *EI*, XIV, pp. 176 f

44. *EI*, II, pp. 116 f

45. *EI*, X, p.17, f

46. *EI*, XIV, pp. 176, f

47. An isolated instance recorded the temple built by Bhoja, *EI*, XVIII, pp. 99 f. Considering the lack of epigraphic evidence M.D. Willis, who negates even the evidence regarding Bhoja, holds that the Pratiharas did not patronise temples at all, preferring instead to confer grants on the brahmanas, 'Religious and Royal Patronage in North India' in *Gods, Guardians and Lovers: Temple Sculptures from North India*, ed. V.N. Desai, and D. Mason, New York, 1993. In Meister and Dhaky et.al, *EITA*, however temple construction is attributed to the patronage of various ruling dynasties including the Pratiharas and dynastic appellations , constitute chapter headings.

48. *EI*, XIV, pp. 176 f

49. *IA*, LVIII, pp. 161 f

50. Ray, H.C. *Dynastic History of Northern India*, II, Calcutta, 1936, p. 1173

51. *EI*, II, pp.116 f

52. *EI*, XXII, pp. 120 f

53. *EI*, III, pp. 263 f

54. *EI*, X, pp. 17f

55. *EI*, XIV, pp. 176f

56. *EI*, II, pp. 116 f.; *IA*, XLII, pp. 57 f

57. *EI*, III, pp. 263 f

58. *IA*, LVIII, pp. 161 f

59. *EI*, XXII, pp. 120 f

60. *EI*, x, pp. 17 f

61. *Supra*

62. *Supra*

63. *EI*, XIV, pp. 176 f

64. *EI*, X, pp.17, f

65. *EI*, XXII, pp. 120 f

66. *Supra*

67. *IA*, LVIII, pp. 116 f

68. *EI*, XXIV, p. 329 f

69. Document VIII, *EI, XXIV*, pp. 329 f

70. *EI*, II, pp. 116 f

72. Pandey, B. K. *Temple Economy Under the Cholas, Delhi*, 1984, pp. 53 f., 103 f

73. *IA*, XIX, pp. 55 f

74. *EI*, XXXV, pp. 55 f

75. *EI*, XXIV, pp. 329 f

76. *EI*, XIV, pp. 176 f

77. *EI*, II, pp.116 f

78. *EI*, III, pp. 263 f

79. *EI*, XXII, pp.120 f

80. The Harsa inscription shows that they renounced all possessions and lived a life of severe austerity. Detailed evidence is presented in the author's forthcoming article on Shaivism

81. *EI*, II, pp. 116 f

82. *EI*, X, pp. 17 f

83. G.H. Ojha, *Udaipur Rājya Kā Itihās,* Ajmer, 1985, p. 130

84. *EI*, XXIV, pp. 329 f

85. The causes for the sustenance of the Kaman grants are further analysed in the author's forthcoming article on Śaivism.

86. *IA*, LVIII, pp. 116 f

87. *EI*, X, pp. 17 f. The inscription states that Muñjarāja destroyed Āghāṭa, the pride of Medapāṭa

88. Sharma, D. *RTA*, p. 248

89. *Pṛthvīrājavijaya*, V. 55-60, D. Sharma, *ECD*, p. 39

90. Ganguly, D.C. 'Ghaznavid Empire' in *The Struggle for Empire* ed. by Majumdar, R.C. Bombay, 1957, p. 10

91. Bhandarkar, D.R *IA*, XLII, pp.116, f

92. No mention is found of any later inscriptions including the Bijolia inscription, A.D. 1170, and the famous work Prithvirajavijaya, which give considerable details regarding the Cahamanas, recording their patronage of the temple, cf. *EI*, XXVI, pp. 102 f.;. Sharma, D. *ECD*, Chap. IV-VII

93. Tod claims having discovered two inscriptions of Laksmana, founder of the Nadol branch, dated v. 1024 , v.1039, *Annals and Antiquities of Rajasthan*, II, pp. 807-8. For further details, see *ECD*, chapter XII

94. The Sūndhā inscription indicates that the Paramāra forces probably occupied Śākaṁbharī for a short while. The defeat by the Mātangas is mentioned by the *Pṛithvīrājavijaya*, v.70, Sharma, D. *ECD*, pp.39-41

Biḍāla-nrisiṁha Temple of Narasinghnath

P.K. Nayak*

Close view of the Biḍāla-nrisiṁha Temple at Narsinghnath, (Orissa)

Narsinghnath is a place of pilgrimage surrounded by dense forest, green mountains and a perennial stream. It is located in the northern slope of the Gandhamardan mountain. The place is at a distance of about 150 kms from Sambalpur town. It is approachable by a good motorable road via Padampur and Paikmal. It is now in Bargarh district of Orissa. Large number of devotees visit the place and pay their homage to *Lord Biḍālanrisiṁha*, the presiding deity of this place. There is an inscription attached to the wall of the *mukhaśālā* which reveals that Baijaladeva, son of Vatsarajadeva, built the temple.[1] The astronomical combinations available in this inscription, when calculated, suggest the date of 1413 A.D. Beglar visited this temple in1974-76 and Bhandarkar in 1904-05.[2]

The temple stands at the foot of the mountain Gandhagiri on the bank of the stream falling down from the mountain. The foundation has been made by cutting the portion of the mountain. The temple is on a platform like structure. The temple has two structures -*Vimāna* and *Jagamohana*. These two are interconnected with an oblong passage which may be taken as an *antarāla*. The *vimāna* is square. The inner size of the *vimāna* is 8'x8' and the platform like structure on which the *sanctum* stands measures 14' x 14'.

*Reader, Dept. of History, Sambalpur University, Orissa

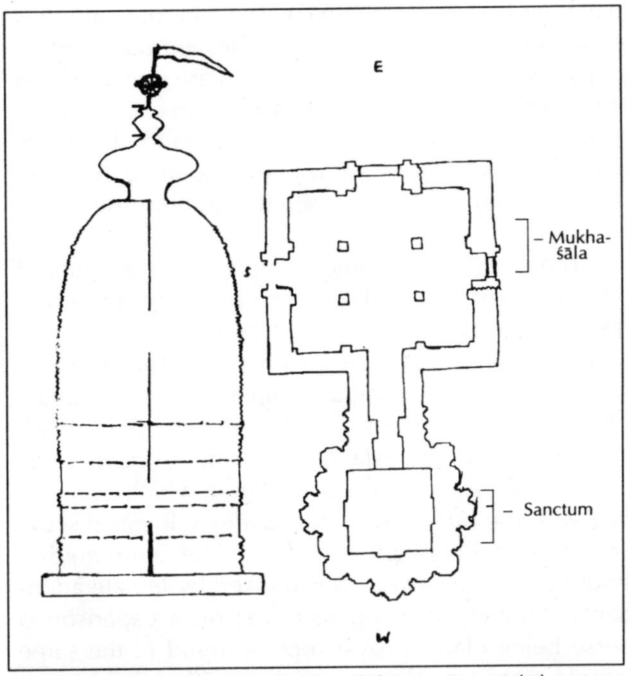

Temple of Biḍāla-nrisiṁha: Line drawing of elevation & ground plan

The height of the *vimāna* from the ground level upto the *kalasha* is 38 feet.[3] The *vimāna (sanctum)* rises straight from the ground. It shows that the importance is not given to the *pishṭa*. Other three usual sections *viz. bada, gaṇḍī* and *mastaka* are clearly visible. The sanctum is square in size and it rises straight upto some height and takes a prominent bend at the top. The *bada* is five fold (*panchanga*) having *pabhāga, tala janghā, bandhana, upara janghā* and *baraṇḍa*. The *pābhāga* consists of five mouldings which are *khura, kuṁbha, pata, kani, basanta*. The *bandhana* which divides the *tala janghā* from *upara janghā* comprises three mouldings of *khura, noli,* and *paṭa*. The *baranda* which terminates the *bada* is composed of seven mouldings which are, from top to bottom, *paṭa, kani, paṭa, noli, paṭa, pheni,* and *khura*. The sanctum is vertically divided into five segments *viz. Kanika, Anuratha, Raha, Anurath* and *Kaṇika. Pīdhāmuṇḍis* are found in the *kaṇika* and *anuratha pagas* of *tala janghā*. The *rahapaga* of *tala janghā* section contains niches where in the *pārsvadevatas* are housed. In the south *Varāha* is installed. North contains *Trivikrama* and west niche is occupied by Nrisiṁha. The image of *Trivikrama* is four armed, out of which one is broken and rest hold conch, discus and mace. In the plaque *Vāmȧna* incarnation with parasol and *kamaṇdalu* is carved in low relief. The figure of king Bali is found there with his minister. Nrisiṁha in the western niche is depicted in *sthānaka* pose with one leg raising upwards from the knee. The god is shown tearing the belly of the demon, who was lying horizontally on the knee. Varāha is depicted in *ālīḍha* pose. The lord is found uplifting the goddess Bhūdevī (earth) from the netherland and placing Bhūdevī on his elbow.

There is an image of Laxmīnarāyaṇa placed into a makeshift niche within the compound. Nārāyaṇa seated in *lalitāsana* embraces his consort in his left arm. The hand of Laxmī is shown around the shoulders of the God. Other sculptures in low relief are found carved on the rock. The important one is that which is now being worshipped as Durgā near the north entrance. The *paga* recesses are filled with the *viralas* and *alasakanyas* or amorous motifs in the lower and upper story. In the upper *janghā* the *pīdhamuṇḍis* are seen. In the *Gaṇḍī* section of *anuratha,* are noticed the *angaśīkharas*. The *raha pagas* are also decorated with the miniature spires but the east *raha* is adorned with a large *śikhara*. The *kaṇika paga* is divided horizontally into a number of *bhūmis* marked by *bhūmiāmalakas*. The *vajramastaka* of *bho* type motifs surmounted by *Gajasiṁha* are placed on the lower *raha* of other sides. The *mastaka* comprises *vedikā* (*bisama*), *beki, āmalaka śilā, khapuri, kalaśa, āyudha* and *dhvaja*. The *āyudhachakra*, was fixed in 1957 A.D. as reported by the temple priests. The principal deity *Marjarakesari* is installed in frontal position in the *sanctum* for which only the face of the cat is visible to the pilgrims/visitors. The hind part is always swathed with cloth and heavy flower coverage. The image of the god is made of black chloride stone. The face is adorned with brass nose, eyes and mouth. The moustache on the face is also clearly discernible. The god is only of its kind in India having such a curious combination.

The *mukhaśālā* or *jagamohana* in front of the *vimana* appears to have undergone heavy modification excepting its fundamental features like four pillars in the centre and the number of pillasters on the inner side walls. The present *jagamohana* is square. It measures 24'x24'. Though the *Jagamohana* is *bhadra deula* comprising *pīḍhas,* it does not provide an elegant elevation due to a stunted height. Originally it was a square structure having four entrances, three on three sides, i.e. east, north and south. The fourth one is in the west connecting the *sanctum.* Now the doorways on the east, north and towards the *sanctum* are present. The southern doorways was probably closed and an alcove was created by masonry work wherein the wooden images of Jagannāth, Subhadrā and Balabhadra are installed. The most striking elements in the *mukhaśālā* are its pillars and the doorways decoration. The pillars are square in cross section and identical in appearance. The shaft of the pillar is square and decorated with demi-lotus medallions intervened with vertical bands of scroll work. At the top, the pillar takes an octagonal shape. The dwarf garland bearers occupy the four corners leaving the four square space. The pillars are crowned with *ghata pallava* capital. The doorframes of the northern and eastern entrance are carved with great care and artistry.

The door jambs of the entrance contain three courses of scroll works *viz. kuṭila, gelaba* and *barajhanjhī.* The *gelaba* band possesses dancing scenes, *liṅga pūjā* in the leafy space and frolicking diminutive human figures. In the *barajhanji* scroll the small citrus amidst the plants are noticed. It is surrounded by the *kutila* bands in which are carved the diminutive elephants along with the *vanalatā.* At the lower part of the jambs are depicted the *dvārapālas.* Gajalaxmī occupies the central place of the lintel where she is shown seated in *lalitāsana* being flanked by elephants above and attendants beneath. The *dvārapālas* wear *jaṭāmukuṭa* and *sarpakuṅḍala.* Both the *dvārapālas, Mahākāla* and *Nandī* are four armed. The *gaṇas* are found attending the both.The usual right hand of *Mahākāla* is in *varada* pose and left hand holds a trident. The upper right catches a rosary and the upper left has a lotus. The main right hand of *nandin* displays *varada* and the corresponding left carries a trident. The upper right hand holds a rosary and the matching left carries a *kapāla.* The face of Nandi has a short beard. In the adjacent niches are sculpted the images of Gaṅgā and Yamunā. Both are standing, two armed and are flanked by parasol bearer. One of the hands is in *kaṭyāvalaṁvita* posture and the other holds a water pitcher. They are mounted on their respective vehicles, i.e., crocodile and tortoise.

The eastern doorframe also contains the figure of *Abhishekalaxmi* seated in *lalitasana* as on the north door. A Navagraha slab is placed on the Gajalaxmi panel. The *dvārapālas* are two handed. They stand in *samabhaṅga* pose being accompanied by the female *chauri* bearers. Besides these, an independent standing figure with moustache is found in *namaskāra mudrā.* It appears to be a royal figure which is identified with the builder king Baijaladeva. It was discovered by D.R. Bhandarkar in 1904.[4] The figure holds a sword against his chest. It is flanked by female attendants. Another royal figure riding on a caparisoned horse being clad in royal rope is found in the same temple premises. The royal figure is attended by two attendants one of which holds a parasol which is above the head of the king. Other attendant is following the horse. This figure is also identified with the statue of king Baijaladeva the builder. This figure is discovered by Dr. N.K. Sahu in 1964. This has been identified with the king Baijaladeva.[5] However, the crescent moon and sun on the top of the slab suggest it to be memorial stone[6], may be of the king. In front of the temple on the other side of the stream is found a Garudastaṁbha.

Besides, these sculptures of the temple there are some sculptures found carved in low relief on the rock towards northern side of the temple. One image of extra large size depicts the image of Gaṇeśa. The image is six armed holding usual objects like rosary, *modaka* etc. He is dancing joyfully. The other one is that of a *dvārapāla* who is standing cross-legged in *bhanga* pose. A long *lakuṭa* placed obliquely is held with his hands. Close to it there is a detached sculpture which represents a female. The local people worship it as Durgā. As told earlier, this image is important. The image is in standing pose. The peculiarity is that the figure places the fingers of the left hand on her *yoni*. It seems to be a representation of a *tāntrik* deity / maiden. On the body of the same rock are engraved a number of seated sculptures of Vishṇu. Higher up on the hill towards the south east of the temple there is a pool on the stream called as 'pandava ghāṭ. There on the rock are found some large sized images carved in a crude manner. People traditionally identify those images with those of Pāndava brothers. These images in fact, are of Brahmā, Vishṇu, Gaṇeśa, Hanumān etc. Brahma is shown seated on his mount swan; Vishṁu is four armed and with his usual features. Hanūmān and Gaṇeśa are also depicted in natural manner.

As mentioned earlier, the presiding deity of this temple is Viḍālanrisiṁha, the cat-lion form of God (the face of cat and the body of the lion). Though the inscriptional chronometry suggest a 15th century date, the architectural fragments, the ornate pillars, highly stylised door frames point to a much earlier date of about 10th /11th century A.D. Very likely there was an old temple there which was completely destroyed in the vagaries of nature. But the place had not lost its religious importance and sacredness. The Chauhan king Baijaladeva, probably catering to the spiritual and religious sentiments of the populace, built the main temple and completely renovated the present *mukhaśālā* which was in an architectural mess. The place name suggests that it was the place of Lord Nrisiṁha. Originally Nrisiṁha was the presiding deity. In this connection it is worth mentioning that a life size image of Nrisiṁha made out of red stone still survives the indifferent care and callous attitude of the temple servants and administration. It is a rare and unique image of Nrisiṃha in royal dignity. It has a face of roaring lion, a human-body and human legs with high boots, a characteristic feature of Sun God. That is why it is taken as a composite image of Sūrya-narasiṁha by Prof. K. K. Dasgupta.[8] The god is flanked by Laxmī on one side and Bhūdevī on the other. Apparently this image was being worshipped in the old temple. Now it is in the kitchen room.

Due to the destruction of the temple and financial constrains, the worship was neglected. In course of time this area was populated largely by the tribals like Sabaras, Kandhas, etc. earlier a known centre of Nrisiṁha worship. The tribals popularised the totemistic worship of cat as their totem in that area before the Chauhan's takeover of the territory. The place Narasinghnath was earlier a known centre of Nrisiṁha worship. The tribals popularised the totemistic worship of cat.

The Chauhan kings were always in favour of reckoning the faith of the people of the locality of their conquered territory. Ramaideva accepted Goddess Patanesvarī, the presiding deity of Patnagarh though he was a devotee of his family deity Ashapurī devī. The Chauhans made it a principle to extol the deities of the people where ever they extended their kingdom. This principle they were following under political expediency and for earning good will of the people. Baijaladeva also faced a similar situation in Narsinghnath. This area, as told earlier, was crowded by the tribal people living with their faith. But this place was the centre of Nrisiṁha worship. Probably the tribals were worshipping the totem of cat. Considering the sentiments of tribal people, the king wanted to satisfy them by acknowledging their faith, i.e., adoration of cat totem. It might have been a political necessity also. To maintain equal status and to vindicate identical respect and reverence to both the cults of Narasiṁha and the totemistic cult of cat worship, Baijaladeva, the Chauhan king thought of a combined mode of worship of both the cults which subsequently emerged as the syncretic cult of Viḍālanrisiṁha. Accordingly, the image of Viḍālanrisiṁha was made with the face of a cat and body of lion. To make it acceptable to Brahmanical fold its origin was attached to Rāmāyaṇa. Viḍāla-nrisiṁha became the presiding deity of the temple. There is a beautiful legend regarding the establishment of the god and the temple. The presiding deity of the temple is described as Viḍālanrisiṁha in the inscription attached to the wall of the *mukhaśālā*. The *Nrisiṁha Charita* a local literary work in Oriya has named the god as *Marjarakesarī* -a composite form of cat and lion, (the head of cat and body of the lion). The *Nrisiṁhacharita* narrates an interesting story about the manifestation of the peculiar incarnation (cat-lion) of lord Vishnu. The story goes like this. A *rishi* named Udaṅga was residing on the bank of the river Godavari. He had a beautiful daughter named Mālatī. Rāvaṇa, the king of Lanka, while traveling, saw Mālatī and was charmed by her beauty. He lost his control and ravished her. The Rishi out of rage cursed the demon king who fled immediately towards his country. Mālatī who was then not in sense, was thrown to the river. River Godavari protected her and brought her back to the bank. When she regained her consciousness, she searched for her father. When she did not get her father, she began to weep being helpless. The weeping of Mālatī was heard by Mushika, the mount of lord Ganeśa. Mushika came to her and assured his help to her but before that he wanted to cohabit her. Thus Mushika had intercourse with her. From this union of Mālatī with Rāvaṇa and Mushika, a demon was born called Mushikadaitya who ate his mother first. Gradually he grew up and performed religious austerities to become invincible. He propitiated Shiva with rigorous penance and obtained the boon from Shiva that he would be victorious over every body except the Lord Nrisiṁha of Satyayuga. Mushika daitya then became all powerful and began to torture all people and gods. The gods being helpless prayed Rāmachandra to protect them. Rāmachandra assumed the form of Narasiṁha and came to the forefront of the demon. The demon seeing Nrisiṁha fled from that place to Gandhagiri, where the present temple stands and prayed him to give shelter. Gandhagiri conceded and the demon went inside the mountain taking the form of a mouse. Narasiṁha assumed the form of cat and continued chasing the demon. Gandhagiri praying the god, intervened the pursuit. The other gods also requested Narasiṁha to establish himself there in that feline form (cat-lion form) and kill the mouse demon when he comes out. Till now the god is waiting there in *Marjarakesarī* form to devour Mushika daitya who has yet to come out of the mountain. The God Narasiṁha waited there in front of the hole of the cave. Gradually the place was covered with thick vegetation. The area was infested by tribals like Sabaras, Kandhas, etc. S.C. Mallick[9] narrates the story about the revelation of the God who had remained underground in the form of Cat-lion, given below.

There were two brothers *kandha* by caste, named Hari and Sahadeva residing in Khandijharan village. Jamunā was the wife of Hari and Rudna was the wife of Sahadeva. They were in the habit of going to the mountain to dig *kanda* (edible roots). One day Jamunā went to Kandagad jharan where she found a big branch of a root. She began to dig. It seemed to her that the *kanda* was as large as the man's body. She continued digging. At last her spade struck the head of the image of Marjarakesarī from which milk came out and filled the cave. A peculiar sound was also heard. Out of fear, Jamunā rushed to her husband and brought him. Hari dug it further and found the image which was seven cubits below the surface. Jamunā carried the image in her basket along with the *kanda* to their house. Hari heard in the dream a voice telling him that the image which he had brought was the image of Narasiṁha who had been there in the shape of a cat to watch the Mushika *daitya*. He was told to worship the image with that *kanda* as *naivedya* (food for God) to the Lord. Hari worshipped first on *baisākha sukla chaturdaṣī* (14th day of bright fort night). That day became the festival day of Narsinghnath belonged to Sabara tribes. This story is narrated in *Nrisiṁha Charita* of Yuga Das[10] in which Hari and Jamunā have been described as Sabar and Sabaruni. The legendary tale has been reiterated in *Nrisiṁha Mahātmya* of Laxmana Mishra Jyotishalankara[11] and published by Sri Rajendra Singh Bariha Bahadur, the chief of Raj Bodasamabar. Another work entitled *Narasiṁha Sāgara* was written by Kandha Kavi Madhusudan Das Bhue. The latest work *Nrisiṁhanath*[13] was authored by Sri Prabhakara Panigrahi in 1974. In every work the same story is told and retold with slight difference.

Places like Savari Nārāyaṅa, Rājim, Pujārīpali, Sīrpur, etc. were famous for Rāma worship. The cult of Rāma was very much popular during the time of Panduvamsis of Srīpura. Later on Narasirṁha became favourite of Soma family as evidenced from the Sīrpur stone inscriptions of Queen Vasata.[14] The cult probably spread towards present Naraingnath area which became a centre of Nrisiṁha worship. Very likely the original temple, remnants of which are traceable in the extant *mukhamaṇḍapa* was dedicated to Lord

Nrisiṁha. Gradually the god was transformed into *Marjarakesarī* due to various circumstantial factors as described above. Due to the influence of the Rāma worship the legendary story was linked with Rāmāyaṇa and Rāma incarnation.

What was the shape of the old temple is difficult to surmise. The present temple, in architectural features and design, is nearer to the style of the temples of Bhuvaneswar and coastal area belonging to the late Ganga period or early Suryavamsi-Gajapati period. In this context the date arrived at through the date of the inscription attached to the *mukhashala* of the temple which points to the 15th century date for the temple, may be accepted safely.

References

1. Mishra, Binayak "Narasimhanath Stone Inscription of Vaij ladeva", *Indian Historical Quarterly*, vol. XII, No.1, 1936, pp.485-486
2. Senapati, N. (ed). *Orissa District Gazetteers* (Samabalpur), Cuttack, 1971 p.532. Beglar, J.D. *Archaeological Survey of India Report* 1874-1875, *Tour in South-Eastern Provinces*, vol. XIII, Varanasi, 1970, pp.140-143
3. *Archaeological Survey of India Report* 1904-05, p.121
4. Senapati, N. (ed), *Orissa District Gazetteers (Sambalpur)*, Cuttack, 1971
5. *Ibid.*
6. T.E. Donaldson, *The Hindu Temple Art of Orissa*, vol. II,, 1986, London, p. 73
7. *Op. cit.*, p.266 Das, D.R. *Temples of Orissa*, Delhi, 1982, pp.31-33
8. Mishra, P.K. (ed) *Culture, Tribal History and Freedom Movement*, Delhi, 1989, pp.137-140
9. Mallick, S.C *History of Patna* 184 B.C. to 1926 A.D. (English, unpublished manuscript), 1926, Acc. No. 52. *Orissa State Archives*, Bhubaneswar, Original vol. I-6, Chapter VI, pp.87-92'i
10. Pruseth, N. (ed) *Nrisiṁha Charita by Yuga Das*, Narsinghnath Temple Management Trust, Narsinghnath, 5th edition, 1993
11. Dash, S.P. *op. cit.*, p.189. The book *Nrisiṁha Mahātmya* was published by Rajendra Singh Bariha in 1908 A.D. (N. Pruseth, *op. cit.*, p.I7)
12. Madhusudan Das Bhue *Narasiṁha Sāgara*, Nrisiṁhanath Temple Management Trust, 1998
13. P. Panigrahi *Nrisiṁhanath*, Sambalpur, 1974
14. *EI.*, vol. XI, pp.I84-201

Pattern of Urban Growth in Northern India during the Sixteenth and Seventeenth Centuries

I.P. Gupta*

The rise of urban settlements in India got an impetus during the second half of the sixteenth century, when Akbar was successful in consolidating the centralized authority and in implementing a systematic political, economic and administrative set up. At the close of the sixteenth century Nizamuddin Ahmed observed in the *Tabaqat-i-Akbar* that there were 120 large cities and 3200 towns *(qasbas)* in the dominion of Akbar.[1] He gives no separate figures for different *subhas* of the empire. However, a large number of contemporary European travellers who visited Indian cities and towns of different regions do provide us with some important statistical information and their impressions about the pattern of urban growth. Similarly, some contemporary or near contemporary Persian sources also furnish valuable information, both statistical and general on cities and towns. For example, *Ain-i-Aikbari, Mirat-i-Ahmedi* and *Kulasat ut-Tawarikh.*

Khulasat-ut Tawarikh mentions that there were cities and towns in every district, *subhas* of Agra and Bengal had very large and flourishing cities and towns.[2] In the *Mirat-i-Ahmedi* there are references to a large number of towns and cities in Gujrat[3] and Thevenot also mentions that Gujrat had a large number of important towns.[4] Similarly Eastern India had many large cities, which witnessed a higher degree of urban growth. The major flourishing cities which witnessed a higher degree of urban growth during this period were Agra, Delhi, Fatehpur Sikri, Lahore Ahmedabad, Thatta, Patna, Dhaka and Burhanpur and very close behind them were the emerging cities with rapid growth such as Ajmer, Multan, Allahabad, Surat, Chanderi, Gwalior, Jagganathpuri, Nasarpur, Sirhind and Mahmudabad. A large number of urban settlements especially the medium sized and small towns of Gujrat, Agra, Bengal, Bihar, Punjab and Sindh *subhas* trace their origin to this period on account of development of textile industries, market facilities and development of inland and foreign trade.

Contemporary travellers who visited the major cities have compared them with London, Paris, Consantinople, etc.

On the basis of size and area and estimates of population mentioned in the contemporary records, we can conclude in making the approximate population of cities and towns given on page 29, indicating the urban growth:

*Former Professor and Head, School of Social Sciences, Central University of Hyderabad

S. No.	Name of Cities/towns	Approximate Size & Area or Circumference	Approximate Population in the 17th Century	Remarks
1.	Agra	36 miles in circumference	6 to 7 lakhs	More than the population of London
2.	Delhi	30 miles in circumference	5 to 6 lakhs (in the second half of the 17th century)	More than the population of Paris
3.	Ahmedabad	More than 30 miles in circumference	5 to 6 lakhs	Growth throughout 16th and 17th century
4.	Lahore	48 miles in circumference by the end of 16th century	5 to 6 lakhs in the beginning of 17th century	Slight decline in comparison to earlier periods in the end of 17th century
5.	Patna	36 miles in circumference	3 to 4 lakhs	Growth
6.	Dhaka	40 miles in circumference	4 to 5 lakhs	Growth
7.	Thatta	One of the largest towns of India	3 lakhs at the close of the 17th century	Growth
8.	Surat	Circumference of about 7 miles	2 to 2.5 lakhs	Growth though fluctuating population
9.	Fatehpur-Sikri	30 miles circumference	3 to 4 lakhs, when it was the imperial capital of the Mughal empire in the 16th century	Capital remained from 3rd July 1573 to March 1586 afterwards population declined
10.	Cambay	Circumference more than Surat say about 8 miles	About 2 lakhs	—
11.	Multan	Moderate size	2,50,000 at the close of the 17th century	—
12.	Burhanpur	14 miles in circumference	2,50,000 (at the close of 17th century)	—
13.	Baroch	4 miles in circumference	1,50,000	—
14.	Ajmer	Of moderate size	About 2 lakhs	When emperor comes, the population increases

Furthermore on the basis of the available records, the main towns of northern India during the sixteenth and seventeenth century have been classified into four categories A, B, C and D and in accordance with their size and population and for their economic and administrative importance. The 'A' category shows major and largest cities. 'B' category shows large towns and 'C', 'D' as medium and small sized towns respectively. The semi-rural-urban towns are placed in 'E' category.

Category of Towns	Ranking Size or Status	Approximate/Range of Population
A Towns	Largest (major cities)	4 lakhs and above
B Towns	Large	1 lakh and above
C Towns	Medium sized	About 50 thousand & above
D Towns	Small	About 10 thousand & above
E Towns	Very small	About 2 thousand & above

List of the classified towns of different categories in the various *subhas* of the Mughal empire is given below:

S. No.	*Subhas*	'A' category	'B' category	'C' category	'D' category	Total
1.	Agra	2	4	21	08	35
2.	Delhi	1	4	09	09	23
3.	Punjab	1	1	07	08	17
4.	Multan	-	2	03	03	08
5.	Sindh (Thatta)	-	4	12	05	21
6.	Kashmir (Sarkar)	-	1	01	05	07
7.	Allahabad	-	3	08	07	18
8.	Oudh	-	2	07	07	16
9.	Bihar	1	2	11	02	16
10.	Bengal	1	8	21	19	49
11.	Orissa	-	2	12	04	18
12.	Gujrat	1	5	25	38	69
13.	Ajmer (Rajputana)	-	1	10	09	20
14.	Malwa	-	4	15	11	30
15.	Khandesh	-	2	09	09	20
16.	Kabul	-	1	03	03	07
		7	46	174	147	374

Classification of Urban Centres

The growth of urban settlements in their size, population and economic activities implies a relationship between population and urban functions. On the basis of certain characteristics and attributes which dominated them, these urban centres can be classified into six groups according to their dominant function *viz.*

i) Centres of administration, ii) Military encampment, iii) Manufacturing Centre, iv) Commercial Centre v) Port town and centre of maritime trade vi) Religious and educational centre.

An attempt has been made here to classify them accurately as far as possible on these lines. A city might originally be established as an administrative centre, but then in due course of time grows into a great commercial or manufacturing city, and *vice-versa*.

Administrative Towns

Administrative towns were the head-quarters of administration of the empire, a *subah* or a *sarkar*. The population in these towns composed of retinues, office clerks, and soldiers stationed here for internal security, law and order and such other duties including the safeguarding of the town itself. Beside various public institutions and religious buildings related to the needs of the public service, *viz.*, schools, *sarais, hamams,* mosques and temples also came up.

Agra though an administrative centre, also became an important commercial and industrial town. Similarly, other towns like Delhi, Ahmedabad and Patna also became commercial and industrial centres. Delhi was one of the resort of Indian and foreign merchants and developed into a great market, as goods were collected here from different parts of the world. Separate markets for every commodity were available here.[5] The textile and dyeing industries were also flourishing and it became a whole sale market for textile goods. It also developed metal industry and other handicrafts.[6]

Ahmedabad was the chief city of Gujrat and during the sixteenth and seventeenth centuries was unsurpassed as a commercial emporium. It was a great market, for different types of commodities, which were collected from different regions of India. There was a great rush of foreign merchants here, including English, Dutch, Portugese, Arabs, Persians and Turks. English, established their factories here. Ahmedabad was a famous market for different varieties of textile goods, indigo, sugar, spices and drugs.[7]

Patna was an important city of eastern India and most famous as centre of commerce and trade, and its market were full of commodities collected here from different regions. The trade was so flourishing here that this city had more than six hundred brokers facilitating the trade[8]. Merchants from foreign countries, Persia, Central Asia, Bhutan and from hilly regions visited it to procure the commodities required in their country. The English and Dutch established their factories here. It was the chief market of agricultural products like food grains, rice, sugar, cotton, spices and other commodities and also for drugs, opium, and salt. Variety of textiles manufactured here had a good market in foreign countries.

Military and Strategic Centres

A number of towns in each region owned their importance to the fact that they were located at strategic points and were fortified ahd powerful garrisons were maintained there. Towns like Allahabad, Ajmer, Gwalior, Ranthambor, Narwar, Chanderi and Mandu come under the category of such towns. These towns though originally established for their strategic or military importance, became important administrative centres later, and developed and expanded rapidly. Allahabad and Ajmer both were important strategic towns, but soon these became administrative centres and the capital of their *subhas* respectively. Towns like Gwalior, Mandu and Ranathambor too had some administrative importance on account of their strategic importance. Such towns, if situated on important trade routes began to develop as commercial centres. Attock an important strategic town became a commercial centre as all the caravans from Persia and other countries of central Asia passed through it. Some of the famous military towns like Bhakkhar which was famous for its fortification and strategic importance also continued to flourish as a large commercial and manufacturing centre. It also developed a great market for the nearby region and also became a famous manufacturing centre.[9]

Commercial Centres

In this category may be included towns which grew up and remained primarily commercial centres. Some of them may have started as administrative or military centres. Towns like Dhaka, Multan, Lahore and Thatta may be included in this category. Rajmahal was formerly the capital of Bengal but when Dhaka developed as a commercial centre it became the capital of the Bengal *subah*. Multan was an old commercial town and a place of great trade, where caravans of merchandise, spices and drugs used to come. Lahore became the seat of Punjab *subah* because it had been a flourishing commercial centre, since very old times. Pelsaert, a Dutch company factor, has mentioned it to be a centre of trade and the English, Armerian and Aleppo merchants did a very profitable business here. Being an important and chief commercial centre, a large number of national and international merchants assembled here.[10] Lahore was a very famous whole-sale market of agricultural commodities and manufactured articles and thus it became a collecting as well as distributing centre of commodities to different regions. Thatta, a great commercial centre afterwards became the administrative centre. Being the centre of great commerce and trade, a large number of foreign merchants established their factories and made huge investments here. It developed important markets of different commodities which catered the demands of local, regional, national and international merchants.

Manufacturing Centres

Most of the towns, which were administrative centres developed local industries and became centres of brisk trade. There were other towns which developed industries and became important on account of local trades and crafts. Benaras, Burhanpur, Dhaka, Baroda, Baroch, besides many more cities were flourishing as manufacturing centres. Benaras was famous for its textiles and fine silk stuffs of various colours worked in gold and silver especially for turbans and girdles which were manufactured here in great abundance.[11] This cloth was distributed all over the regions of the Mughal Empire. Metal utensils including those intended for domestic use were manufactured in large quantities and sent to different regions. Dhaka was famous for textiles especially muslin and silks which were sent to national and international markets. Boats were also manufactured and jute industry was also flourishing. Burhanpur was famous for its textile industries which were manufactured here in exceeding fine muslin for women's headdresses and was in great demand in foreign countries.[12] It seems that a number of iron factories existed there. Baroda and Baroch too were great manufacturing centres.

In addition to the major industrial towns, smaller towns produced manufactured goods for local markets while the others for a wider market, national or international. Among such important industrial towns were Srinagar, Sialkot, Sirhind, Samanah, Nasarpur, Sahwan, Pattan, Sironj, Nosari, Atwal, Bharatpur, Biana, Jaunpur, Shahzadpur, Gaya, Sonergaon, and Malda.

Port Towns

India has been connected with foreign countries by sea routes from time immemorial and port towns are consequently very old having been centres of overseas and coastal trade from ancient times. Some of the important port towns of the country were Cambay, Surat, Baroch, Dhaka, Lahri Bandar, Reanmundy, Angeli, Balasore, Hughly, Rajmahal, Chattagong located in different regions of the country. The prosperity of a port town depended on its hinterland, facility of communications with the interior and the location of the harbour. When the sea was close to Cambay, it was a very good port as vessels reached the town directly but when the sea receded, it resulted in an immense loss to the port of Cambay.[13] A convenient base for loading and unloading the goods from the ships, excellent water or road communication for collecting and dispatching the goods to distant places further added to the growth of such towns. This was essentially the case with the port of Surat. Surat had a good harbour and had also a convenient base for collecting goods for export as it was well connected by roads with the different regions. Goods produced in the empire of the Mughals, kingdom of Golconda and Bijapur reached Surat to be exported by sea to different countries of Asia and Europe.[14] The other port towns like Baroch, Hughli, Rajmahal and Lahri Bander had many geographical and economic advantages which enhanced their importance as port towns. The ports of Angeli[15], Balasore, Hughli, Chittagong[16] and Lahari Bander were similarly very busy centres of overseas trade.

The Indian cities and towns had an economic viability with strong economic base. All major cities developed multifunctional character and these were not merely camp towns, as Bernier and Thevenot have mentioned. It will not be out of place that this urban growth, resulted in bringing urbanization in Indian sub-continent during seventeenth century. The urbanization was of greater intensity in the coastal regions *viz.* Bengal and Gujarat and in the proximity of junction of trade routes *viz.*, Punjab, Multan and Sindh. The urbanization transformed and brought socio-economic and cultural development in the country.

References

1. Nizamuddin Ahmed *Tabaqat-i-Akbar*, Elliot and Dowson, ed. *History of India as Told by its own Historians*, vol.V, London, 1867-77, pp.106-107
2. Sujan Rai *Khulasat-ut-Tawarikh* tr. *Topographical Introduction*, J. N. Sarkar, included in his 'India of Aurangazeb', Calcutta, 1921, pp.40-41
3. Ali Muhammad Khan *Mirat-i-Ahmadi*, (supplement) tr by M.F.Lokhandwala, Baroda, 1965, pp.14-18 and 153
4. Jean de Thevenot *'Relation de l'Indiston*, 1666-67. Levell's tr. of 1687 reprinted with notes and introduction by Surendernath Sen in the *The Indian Travels of Thevenot and Careri*, New Delhi, 1949, p.46
5. Bernier, F. *Travels in the Mogul Empire*, tr. by A. Constable, revised and ed. by V. A. Smith, London, 1934
6. *Ibid.*, pp. 254 & 255
7. Mandelslo *Travels in Western India* (1638-39), Oxford University Press, London, 1931, p.8
8. Manrique, F.S. *Travels (1629-43)* tr C. E. Luard, assisted by Hosten, 2 vols, Haklunyt Society, London, 1927, vol.2, p.146
9. Peter Mundy *'Travels'*, vol.II, p.157 in *Travels in Asia 1630-34*, ed. R.C.Temple, Hakluyt Society, London, 1914, second series, XXXV
10. Pelsaest, *Franscisco Remonstrantie*, tr. by Moreland and Geye, *Jahangir's India*, Cambridge, 1925, p.44
Terry , p.14, *E.F.R.* vol. VI., p.135
11. Manrique, F.S. *op.cit.*, p. 147
12. Tavernier, *op.cit.*, vol. I, p.51; Manrique, *op.cit.*, vol. II, p.429
13. Thevenot, *op.cit.*, p.18
14. Tavernier, *op.cit.*, vol. I, p.35
15. Ralph, Fitch, *Narrative*, ed, J. H. Ryley *England's Pioneers to India and Burma*, London, 1899, p.115
16. Abul Fazal *Ain-i-Akbari* tr. by Jarret vol. II, Calcutta, 1927-39, p.137

The Aḷvar Movement in Kerala

Gopi Krishnan G.*

An attempt has been made here to bring out the historical significance of the Vaishṇava devotional movement led by the aḷvar saints which flourished in the Chera country (Kerala) and in the Ay chiefdom. Kerala in the past was known as *malaināḍu* and the Ay chiefdom included the present Kanyakumari district of Tamilnadu which was earlier called as *nanchināḍu.* The study focuses on the main peculiarities of the early Vaishṇava movement in Kerala and the contributions of Kerala to the south Indian Vaishṇavism. Also, it analyses the role played by the Vaishṇava *divyadesams* or the early Vaishṇava shrines in the early medieval history of Kerala and the impacts of the *aḷvar* movement on its culture. The period covered in the study is the three centuries, from the eighth century A.D. to the eleventh century A.D.

The study is based on primary records such as the *Nalayiram Divya Prabandham, the Travancore Archaeological Series,* and *Epigraphia Indica.* Vaishṇavism received a new impetus in the sixth century A.D. in south India when a group of twelve saintly persons, popularly known as the aḷvar, took up its leadership and started preaching an emotional Vaishṇava religion based on *bhakti* or devotion.[1] The aḷvar came one after another, covering the period of the four centuries from the sixth century A.D. Hence, the period witnessed the growth of Vaishṇava *bhakti* movement resulting in the emergence of popular Vaishanavism.[2] The same period saw the origin and development of Śaiva devotional movement led by the *nayanars* in South India. It is argued that the word aḷvar means' one who delves deep into the ocean of devotion' which denotes the deepest form of devotion. Similarly, it is held that the word stands for the Vaishṇava concept of 'preservation'. However, the most acceptable view is that the word *aḷvar* originated from the Tamil root *al* which means one who shares or possesses the wealth of the master. Significantly, the sanskrit word *bhakta* has also the same connotation.[3]

The twelve aḷvar were Poigai Aḷvar, Putattalvar, Peyalvar (they are the earliest saints known as mudalalvars), Tirumalisai Aḷvar, Tirppanalvar, Tondradippodi Aḷvar, Tirumangai Aḷvar, Kulasekhara Aḷvar, Periyalvar, Andal, Nammalvar and Madurakavi.[4] The aḷvars identified one hundred and eight Vaishṇava shrines as the holy places or *divyadesams* on which centered their bhakti movement. The aḷvars took out grand pilgrimages to these shrines. They moved singing and dancing. The aḷvar movement

*Department of History, University of Calicut, Kozhikode

originated in the Pallava country and gradually but swiftly it spread to the Chola country. Soon the wave of Vaishṇava devotionalism found its way to the Pandyan and from where finally it reached the Chera country and the Ay chiefdoms.[5]

The aḷvar Vaishṇavism began to flourish in the Chera-Ay lands. These monarchs, especially the Cheras, wholeheartedly espoused the cause of Vaishṇavism though the 'Siva devotionalism had reached the Chera country earlier. The royal patronage that the aḷvar movement received gave a fillip to Vaishṇavism in Kerala. Only the three aḷvar Thirumangai Aḷvar, Kulasekhara Aḷvar and Nammaḷvar paid visits to the *divyadesams* of Kerala and started preaching Vaishṇava devotionalism. They were responsible for the spread of Vaishṇavism in Kerala. The aḷvars soon identified thirteen Vaishṇava shrines spread over the Chera and Ay lands as the *divyadesams* and centered their movement on these shrines. The *divyadesams* of Kerala are- Thirppathisaaram, Thirvattaru, Thiruvananthapuram, Thiruchenkannur, Thirvanvandur, Thirukkodithanam, Thirukkakara, Thrimulikkulam, Thirumutakkodu and Thirunava.[7] Among these temples, the first three belonged to the Ay chiefdom while the rest were within the Chera country. Thirumangai Aḷvar had composed songs or *Pasurams* on Thiruvalla, Thirumulikkulam and Thirumuttavakkodu in his *periya tirumoli* while Kulasekhara aḷvar in his *perumal tirumoli* praised only one *divyadesam* of Kerala, i.e., Tirumuttakkodu. But, Nammavar had composed songs on twelve of these shrines except Thirumuttakkodu. Since the date of these aḷvar have been fixed between the eighth and the tenth centuries, it is clear that the aḷvar movement was active in Kerala in the same period.[8]

The *pasurams* or the songs composed by the aḷvars provide information regarding the socio-economic background of the *divyadesams*. The aḷvars narrated the *divyadesams* of Kerala as the centres of Vedic Brahmins who performed sacrifices and engaged in chanting of Vedic hymns. The *pasurams* give the information regarding the agrarian background and the environmental features of the places where the *divyadesams* were situated. Many of the *divyadesams* of Kerala were said to have existed in the midst of vast fields of cultivable lands where agricultural items such as arecanut, coconut, sugarcane, etc. grew in large numbers.[9]

This shows that the *divyadesams* like the temples of the period encouraged agriculture and relied on it for survival. Also, the *divyadesams* seemed to have flourished during the period.

Similarly, by the eighth century A.D., the newly arrived Brahmins had settled in thirty two villages known as *grāmas* and began to spread to the new sub-settlements. Three shrines, among the *divyadesams,* namely Thiruaranmula, Thiruvalla and Thirumulikkulam were also *grāmakshetras* of the respective settlements.[10] Significantly, Thirumulikkulam was a prominent temple which seated the headquarters of a *tatiathiri or taliadhikari* or one of the four executive committee members elected from the Brahmins of the Chera country to form an advisory council to advise and check the Chera monarch.[11] The Thirumulikkulam temple had occupied an important place in the history of Kerala. The *mulikkulam kachcham,* the first known *devaswom* regulation in Kerala, was ratified by the socio-political leadership of the time at the Mulikkulam temple. This *kachcham* was repeatedly mentioned in the temple documents of the early medieval period which was regarded as an inviolable charter. The *divyadesams* of Kerala as the other temples of the early medieval period rose to prominence in the socio-political set up of the time. It is evident from the inscriptions found in the various *divyadesams.* The Thiruvanvandur and Thrikkodithanam temple inscriptions speak about donations of certain landed properties to these temples and the arrangements made for its protection and maintenance.[12] Similarly, the Thiruvalla inscriptions provide information about the place of a temple in the early medieval Kerala. These epigraphs elaborate the functions to be performed by various temple servants ranging from the chief priest to the watchman, the details of the donations of landed properties to the *devaswom* for various purposes and the steps to maintain the *devaswom* properties and the celebration of the *Onam* festival.[13] Also, the Thrikkakara inscriptions provide enough information regarding the place of that temple in the Chera and the post - Chera period.[14] Thus, from the study of these inscriptions it is clear that the *divyadesams* of Kerala flourished during the Chera period which is a pointer to the fact that the Chera rulers upheld the Vaishṇava religion, though they encouraged Śaivism too. The vast landed properties were donated to the *divyadesams*. The prosperity of these shrines was mainly due to the flow of wealth and royal patronage. The Chera rulers were great builders and patrons of temples who started constructing a large number of structural temples.[15] It seemed that the *divyadesams* of Kerala were structurally transformed during the Chera ascendancy. Also the Ay rulers of southern Kerala built many structural temples and patronised Vaishṇava faith though some of the rulers of this line were vehement advocates of Buddhism.[16] So it is probable that the three *divyadesams* which fall in the Ay chiefdom were renovated or built structurally by the Ay rulers. The aḷvar movement was the second major civilising agent in Kerala after the spread of the Brahmins. While the latter mainly came from Tulunadu, the aḷvar movement arrived from the Tamil mainland and it brought Tamil culture to Kerala which greatly influenced the Brahmins.

The agrarian centered groups wholeheartedly encouraged aḷvar Vaishṇavism. It is clear from the donation of landed properties to the *divyadesams* by the wealthy agriculturists. But in the later period the traders also began to patronise Vaishṇavism. As a result the trusteeship was accorded to the *manigrāmam* traders in various temples. The same trend existed in the Pallava-Chola-Pandyan territories where the trading class stood with Buddhist and Jain sects during the early phase of aḷvarism.

Kerala's role in the development of south Indian Vaishṇavism was immense. Kulasekhara aḷvar was the greatest contribution of Kerala to the south Indian Vaishṇavism and he was responsible for the spread of aḷvar Vaishṇavism in the early medieval Kerala. He was the reigning monarch and was identified as Sthanu Ravi who ruled the Chera country from A.D. 844 to A.D. 883.[17] He had composed *Perumal thirumoli* which consisted of one hundred and five hymns. It is included in the *Nalayiram Divya Prabandham,* a compilation of the *pasurams* or songs composed by the aḷvars. Kulasekhara Aḷvar had praised eight *divyadesams* in *Perumal thirumoli.*[18] It is believed that he gave his daughter to the service of Sri Rangam temple and donated much of his wealth to that temple. The Aḷvar also composed a *stotra* namely *mukundamala* which was quoted in the preface of a Vaishṇava epigraph at Pagan in Burma.[19] Similarly, an inscription of the Chola king Kulothunga I speaks about the provisions for the recital of *terrarum tiral,* a part of *Perumal Tirumoli* at Sri Rangam.[20]

Further, a temple for Kulasekhara aḷvar was constructed by the Vaishṇavites at Mannarkovil in southern Tamil Nadu.[21] Thus, it is clear that Kulasekhara Aḷvar was a great Vaishṇava saint dedicated his life for the popularisation of Vaishṇavism in the entire Tamilakam. The Vaishṇavites have a *vandanasloka* in which they venerates the memory of the aḷvar. Thirukkulasekharapuram Vishṇu temple, though it was not included in the traditional list of the one hundred and eight *divyadesams,* was one of the prominent Vishṇu temples of Kulasekhara aḷvar's period. It is generally held that the aḷvar composed *mukundamala* in praise of the deity of this temple.

Significantly, Vaishṇava-Śaiva conflict was absent in Kerala even when the aḷvar -nayanar movements reached the zenith of their activities. In the other parts of south India, the Vaishṇavites and the Śaivites engaged in struggles for supremacy.

The aḷvar movement greatly influenced the culture of Kerala. One of the greatest impacts of the movement was the popularisation of the Onam festival in Kerala.[22] For this, the aḷvars did not contribute directly. Along with the development of devotionalism on a large scale, many temple festivals became popular festivities in south India during the aḷvars' period. Also, the popular festivals were being systematically used by the preachers of devotionalism to attract more people to their fold. The Thiruvalla copper plates indicate how the Onam was celebrated in that temple.[23] The royal patronage was also given to this festival. The Thiruvattuvay inscription also makes reference to the Onam festival. As a result of the spread of aḷvar Vaishṇavism, Onam was developed into a most popular festival of Kerala from a mere Vaishṇava ceremony.

Similarly, the Malayalam new year festival, *Vishu* also developed in the Vaishṇava temples. One of the Thrikkadithanam temple inscriptions refers to the celebration of *Vishu*.[24] Thus the two popular festivals of Kerala developed on Vaishṇava background in the Chera period when the aḷvars vociferously preached the Vaishṇava religion and popularised everything connected with Vaishṇavism.

The aḷvar movement resulted in the construction of many structural temples in Kerala. Besides the thirteen *divyadesams,* a good number of Vaishṇava temples were built in structural pattern in many parts of Kerala. The Ay rulers built Parthivapuram temple and patronised Vaishṇavism. Similarly, many Vaishṇava temples, such as the Varkala temple, Thirukulasekharapuram and Kudal Manikkam were built or structurally renovated during the Chera period. The Mushaka kings also followed the suit and constructed Vishṇu shrines such as the Trichambaram and Narayanapuram temples.[25] Thus the entire Kerala was influenced by Vaishṇava religion during the early medieval period mainly due to the works done by the aḷvar saints. Kings like Sthanu Ravi embraced the cause of aḷvarism and himself became an aḷvar, perhaps as a policy of expediency. The royal patronage boosted the aḷvar movement in Kerala.

The literature of the period was greatly influenced by aḷvar Vaishṇavism. Besides, the *Perumal thirumozhi* and *Mukundamala,* Kulashekhara aḷvar authored three Sanskrit dramas *Subhadhradhananjayam, Thapathisamvaranam* and *Vischinnabhishekam* and a prose work called *Ascharyamanjari*. Significantly, the aḷvar Vaishṇavism influenced Saktibhadra, who wrote the first full scale Sanskrit drama of south India, *Ascharyachoodamani*.[26] The aḷvar movement was responsible for the spread of Vaishṇavism in Kerala which influenced and enriched the various fields of literature during the Chera period. The aḷvars popularised the Vaishṇava legends and Purāṇas in Kerala which in later years led to the composing of many medieval works having the story of Rāmāyana or Bhāgavatha as main themes.

In fact, the aḷvars' activities resulted in the popularisation of Vaishṇavism in Kerala in a big way. Until that time, Vaishṇava religion might be limited to the Nambudiri Brahmins and their centres. But, Vaishṇava faith got a cosmopolitan out look and more sociability in Kerala after the advent of the aḷvar movement. The same trend had happened in Tamil main land also.[27]

The Buddhist and Jain schools lost popular support when Vaishnavaism arrived with a more popular base using dancing, singing and grand pilgrimages as methods to spread the religion.[28] Significantly, among the aḷvars who worked in Kerala belonged to the non-Brahmin and the so-called lower strata of the society. Thirumangai aḷvar belonged to the Kallar Community and Nammaḷvar was a vellala by birth. This, again might be a factor for the reunion of many of those non-Brahmins who embraced Buddhist or Jain schools of Hindu religion. Thus, the aḷvar movement was one of the major reasons for the speedy decline in the popular support of Buddhism and Jainism. So more visibly, the spread of Vaishṇava religion was the major impact of the aḷvar movement in Kerala.

Further, the aḷvars acted as the agents of cultural integration and unity. They could visit various political entities of the time without any obstacles. They moved freely spreading the Vaishṇava ethos, especially the Krishṇa and Rāma devotionalism. This free movement helped in bringing out a sense of unity in cultural terms. The pilgrimages to various *divyadesams* spreading over various parts of south India further cements this process. The *divyadesams* of Kerala were frequently visited by the Vaishṇavites from Tamilakam and the Vaishṇava devotees from Kerala paid visits to the Vaishṇava shrines of the other parts of south India. This brought out a strong cultural interlinking between Kerala and other parts of south India.

Similarly, the aļvar movement was indebted to the traders for its speedy growth since the trade routes which connected various parts of south India were the only means of conveyance available to the aļvar saints. The exchange routes were used by the saints to reach the *divyadesmas* of Kerala. Further, many exchange routes might have been newly carved out or cleared as a result of the frequent movement of the aļvars and the bandwagon of their devotees. The Mekkarai pass of the western ghats linking the southern parts of the Pandyan kingdom and the Chera country is one such exchange route. This route became famous as 'Achankovil Pass'.[29] In later years, many fugitives from the Pandyan kingdom reached the Achankovil river valley through this pass. Significantly, the development of a cluster of six *divyadesams* in the central Travancore (parts of modern Pathanamthitta, Alapuzha and Kottayam districts of Kerala) was the direct result of the Achankovil Pass being used by the aļvars. The route coming through the Achankovil Pass led to Chengannur around which place the six *divyadesams* flourished. Significantly one of the *Keralopathis* says that Chengannur witnessed a major Tamil influx in the past.[30] Similarly, the early Vaishṇava centres of Kerala are situated on the nearby areas of the major exchange routes coming from Tamil Nadu. The *divyadesams* of the southern parts of the Ay chiefdom were situated near the exchange routes leading from the Aramboli Pass. Thus the early Vaishṇava centres originated near the inter-regional and the intraregional exchange routes. So the commercial activities and the Vaishṇava devotional movement helped each other in the course of each ones' development. Also, the frequent movement of people through certain particular routes led to the advent of many local markets and semi-towns.

Thus, the aļvar movement was one of the major civilising agents in the early medieval Kerala. It influenced and enriched the society and culture of Kerala.

References

1. Narayanan, M.G.S. *Foundations of South Indian Society and Culture*,New Delhi, 1994, p. 190
2. Sirnivasa Aiyangar, M. *Tamil Studies,* New Delhi, 1986, p. 291
3. Narayanan, M.G.S. *op.cit.*, p. 191
4. Gopinatha Rao, T.A. *History of Srivaishnavas,* Madras, 1923, pp. 2-7
5. Narayanan, M.G.S. *op. cit.*, pp. 192-194
6. Narayanan, M.G.S. *The Perumals of Kerala,* Calicut, 1996, pp. 188-189
7. *Ibid.*
8. *Ibid.*
9. Venkataswamy Reddiyar, K. (ed.) *Nalayira Divya Prabandham,* Chennai, 1981, *pasurams,* 2843-2853 (*pasurams* on the Thiruaranmula temple) and Raghava Aiyangar, M. *Ceravendar Ceyyutkovai* (compiled), Trivandrum, 1951, pp. 3-54 and pp. 214-277 (*pasurams* by the aļvars on the *divyadesams* of Kerala)
10. Kesavan Veluthat, *Brahmin Settlements in Kerala,* Calicut, 1978, pp. 21-32
11. Narayanan, M.G.S, *op.cit.*, p. 86
12. *Travancore Archaeological Series,* vol. II, pp. 33-45
13. *Travancore Archaeological Series,* vol. II, part III, .pp. 131-207
14. *Travancore Archaeological Series,* vol. III, pp. 173-188
15. Elamkulam P.N. Kunjan Pillai, *Studies in Kerala History,* Trivandrum, 1970, p. 325
16. *Ibid.*, pp. 173-182
18. M. Srinivasa Aiyangar, *op.cit.*, p. 21
19. It is a Tamil inscription of the thirteenth century speaking about an endowment for a permanent lamp in a *mandapa* to be constructed at the Vishṇu temple at Pagan by one Ryirian Cirian alias Kulasekhara Nambi of Makotaiyar Patnam in *malai mandalam. Epigraphia Indica,* vol. III, p.197
20. *South Indian Inscriptions,* vol. III, p. 148

21. K. K. Raja, *The Contributions of Kerala to Sanskrit Literature,* 1958, p. 2

22. Elamkulam P.N. Kunjan Pillai, "Onam charithrathil", *Samskara Kairali,* September-October 2002, Tiruvananthapuram

23. *Tranvancore Archaeological Series,* vol. II, part III, pp.131-207

24. *Travancore Archaeological Series,* vol. II, pp. 33-45

25. Unni, N.P. *A History of Mushikavamsa,* Trivandrum, 1980, pp. 181-183

26. The stories from the Rāmāyana were taken as the theme of this drama by Saktibhadra.
Also Fr. Kamil Bulcke, *Ramakathā,* Trichur, 1978, p. 201

27. Narayanan, M.G.S. *Foundations of South Indian Society and Culture,* New Delhi, 1994, pp. 210-214

28. *Ibid.,* pp. 206-208

29. Caldwell Bishop, *History of Tinnevelly,* New Delhi, 1982, p. 25

30. Gundert, (ed.) *Keralopathi,* Trivandrum, 1961, p. 16

Tawaif and Khawas in the Hyderabad State: A Gender Perspective

Vandana Kaushik*

Search for gender perspectives in the history of the eighteenth and early nineteenth century Hyderabad poses many problems. First, history writing had revolved around political events which were mostly out side the domain of women. Hence, they were marginalised. They find space in the social and cultural history but there also they are the subject of narration. The processes of political, social and economic changes happening around them would surely have influenced them. But the changes in the circumstances or their conditions did not mean that they had any say in it or were involved in the process of change as an instrument. Secondly, all Persian court-records, daily diaries, newsletters, or Deccani Masanavis (long poems) were written by men. Hence, it was natural for them to write about the matters which interested them or concerned them. Women and their feminine pursuits might have amused them, entertained them but were not considered to be worthy of serious concern or attention. The institutions those of *khawas* (concubine) and *tawaif* (courtesan) definitely interested them because they reinforced their image of power and control over them. Hence, during eighteenth century and in the early nineteenth century, we find continuous references of them in contemporary chronicles. Their presence is reported in all the ceremonies, festivals, and court-scenes. *Tawaifs* were not necessarily involved in the flesh trade. They lived by their profession of singing and dancing and had independent source of income. They were an integral part of the aristocratic classes. In contrast, *khawas* of the royal harem had no life outside it. In the eighteenth century, *khawas* or *tawaif* was not a derogatory term.

The struggle between the Nizam, the Marathas, the East India Company and the Mysore State had a direct bearing on the institutions of the *tawaif* and *khawas*. Nizam-ul-Mulk Asaf Jah Ist was not only the founder of the State, but was also the most powerful of the successive Nizams. Hence, he had laid down rules for *tawaifs* in his court. These rules were recorded by his secretary Lala Mansaram in *Zawabit-i-Huzur Purnoor* in 1762 A.D. According to Lala Mansaram, nobles could have singing and dancing parties only on specified occasions such as Id or marriages only and that too only in their homes and with prior permission of the Daroga (police superintendent).[1] Prostitutes were not allowed to live inside the city. Nobody was allowed to enter the city in a drunk-

*Reader, History Dept. , SPM College, Delhi University, New Delhi

en state from the house of a prostitute.[2] There is hardly any reference of *khawas,* in the records of the 1st Nizam's period.

Nizam-ul-Mulk Asaf Jah Ist died in 1748 and after a period of instability, his son Nizam Ali Khan became the second Asaf Jah in 1761. This was a period of continuous warfare, femine, and the loss of political power which resulted in the subsidiary treaty between the Nizam and the East India Company in 1798. Interestingly, during these years the number of *khawases* and *tawaifs* increased in Hyderabad. Nizam Ali Khan had shifted his capital from Aurangabad to Hyderabad in 1777, and ruled till 1803. His court was full of painters, singers, dancers, and poets. At the same time, the power of the nobles also increased. The Nizam allowed them to use the privileges which were hitherto forbidden by the 1st Nizam, such as the use of *palaki, naqqara* (a kettle drum) and naubat[3] (a set of kettle drums, struck at stated intervals in front (sic) of the palace of the king or prince, or the recipient of the privilege). Instead, one finds Nizam Ali Khan himself gifting these as honours to some of his nobles[4] and *tawaifs* such as Mahalaqa Bai Chanda who was bestowed with the title *Saheb-i-Naubat.*[5]

Mahalaqa Bai Chanda's life history presents an interesting example of social mobility among *tawaifs.* She came from a humble background as her mother had a hard time in raising her three daughters. They were all beautiful and accomplished singers and dancers. Thus, they became *tawaifs* and enjoyed high status among the aristocracy. They changed their names and Mahalaqa Bai's mother Maida Bibi became Raj Kunwar bai, as the word *'kunwar'* gave her respectability.[6] Mahalaqa Bai was equally favoured by the Nizam and his Minister Mir Alam. Her regular presence in the court of Nizam Ali Khan, is recorded in the newsletters of Hyderabad. According to the report of *Akbar-i-Durbar-i-Daulat Madar,* 29 Muharram, 1209 Hizari (News-letter of Hyderabad dated 26th August 1794) she attended the court and complained that she had not received her allowances since the last three months.[7] This incident shows that *tawaifs* were granted regular allowances and they were conscious of their rights.

Tawaifs were part of the social life of aristocracy whereas *khawases* had their place only in *zanana.* During the last decades of the eighteenth century, contemporary records refer to sudden increase in the number of *khawases* in the royal harem. Who were these girls? How all of a sudden there were thousands of girls in the palace. Who brought them and what was their reaction? Some answers can be searched in the famine of 1792-96. As it was one of the worst famine, people of Telangana were forced to sell their children. These children especially the girls were bought by the State. Mudiraj K. Krishnaswamy recorded in the 'Pictorial Hyderabad' as follows:

' Nizam Ali Khan had two battalions consisting of one thousand each, of women which were picked mainly from the classes of Dher and Chamar, played a very conspicuous and gallant part against the enemies of the Nizam.'[8]

Being dependent for grain on rural agricultural classes, *Dher* and *Chamar* would have been the worst affected by the famine. Theses girls thus purchased during the long spell of the famine were trained in tailoring and other crafts such as coppersmith and goldsmith.[9] Large number of girls found themselves inside the harem where except the Nizam, no other male member above the age of 7 years was permitted to enter.[10] Shah Kamtar completed a *Masanavi* in Deccani Urdu in 1807. He recorded that ' the Nizam had a new khawas as concubine every night whom he himself decorated as bride'[11] Najmul Ghani Khan wrote in the *Tarikh-i-Riysat-i-Deccan* in 1930 quoting from the *Tarikh-i-Khursheed-Jahi* that people themselves used to send their girls to the Nizam's harem to cheer him up as he was feeling depressed because of the death of his son where some of them could find their way to his bed also.[12]

These instances provide a glimpse of the society where women were being used merely as sex objects. We hardly find any reference of their resistance or revolt. Contemporary sources do not refer to any resistance. Either there was none or no one was there to record them. As referred to earlier, all authors were men. Second explanation seems more plausible. Harem life provided financial security, social prestige and sometimes even legal status. Once inside the harem and after acquiring certain position in the *zanana,* they lived luxurious life, rode elephants, and accompanied the Nizam even in the hunting parties. They were provided with liberal allowances.[13]

During the reign of Afzal-ud-Dowla, the fifth Nizam, the practice of finding favours and getting allowances through sending girls in the harem continued. Nawab Server-ul-Mulk reached Hyderabad from Delhi after 1857. He wrote his autobiography in Urdu which was translated by his son Nawab Jiwan-Yar Jung . He has narrated an incident when one hakim named Raza Ali Khan wanted to get a manasab from the 5th Nizam Afzal-ud-Dowla by sending his niece to his harem through a Sufi saint Noor-ud-Din Shah Kadari who had influence with the Nizam. But the octarian Sufi became infatuated with the girl and himself married with her. Her uncle received a mansab of Rs. 80 per month.[14] Lines between legitimate and other wise were not so deep or clearly drawn. These girls from the poor families could live a luxurious life and become a part of the social elite group if they could find favours with the Nizam. Henery Briggs wrote in 1861 about Secunder Jah the 3rd Nizam in the following words:

'Secunder Jah has been called illegitimate, but the expression is wrongly applied in respect of Asopheea family; for the reigning prince, while he has unrestricted commerce with any female on the premises of his palace, the moment she becomes pregnant, he undergoes with her the legal obligation of nikah, which gives legitimacy to the issue. This I may mention, is a common custom in all Mohammedan countries, and the intervention of the Cazee is not even required; two witnesses also to be Mohammmedan being sufficient to verify and make valid the *nikah.*'[15]

Once inside royal *zanana* these women zealously guarded their financial interests. In the 19th century when they found that their allowances could be adversely affected by the removal of Salar Jung, the minister, they intervened in his favour. Syed Husain Bilgrami, the private secretary of Salar Jung I wrote in ' A memoirs of Sir Salar Jung'

'In connection with the temporary estrangement between the Nizam and his Minister, it is worth mentioning that the ladies of His Highness's harem and those of his predecessors, who all reside in the Palace, threatened to rebel if the Minister was dismissed. They said that since he had been in office, their pensions and allowances were paid punctually. They had never been so under previous Ministers. The ladies therefore, allied themselves to the Minister's cause and would not hear of his dismissal. This specific circumstance is worth mentioning although it is by no means the first occasion on which the ladies of the Nizam's household have proved themselves to be very important factors in the Haiderabad politics.'[16]

Thus, the picture which emerges from the contemporary sources is of a society submerged in the pleasures of senses because deep inside, the Nizam, the nobility, gentry all were hurt, resentful and helpless as the real power had passed into the hands of the East India Company and its Resident at Hyderabad. Life was easy and gay for the high classes and *tawaifs* could marry into the aristocracy and thus enter the *zanana.* However, once a part of the *zanana,* she could not leave as she wished. *Tawaif* could become *khawas* and not the vice-versa. *Tawaif* and *khawas* were two institutions of the Hyderabad which were integral part of the life of the Nizam and his nobles.

References

1. Manasaram Lala *Zawabit-i-Huzoor* Pur Noor, Persian Manuscript completed in 1762, Osmania University Library, Hyderabad, No. 841, p.12

2. *Iibid.*, p.46

3. *Ibid.*, p.11

4. Gulam Imam *Tarikh-i-Khursheed Jahi,* Persian Manuscript completed in 1872 Salar Jung Museum Library (henceforth SJML) no.170, p.291

5. Muhammad Abdul Aziz *Tarikh-i-Aziz-i-Deccan,* (printed Urdu), Kanpur, 1887, p.72

6. Gulam Samadani *Hayat-i-Mahlaqa,* (printed Urdu), Hyderabad, 1906, pp.7-8

7. *Akhabari-i-Durbar-i-Daulat* Madar, 29 Muharram, 1209, No.2, 361.9, Andhra Pradesh State Archives, Hyderabad

8. Mudiraj K. Krishna Swamy *Pictorial Hyderabad,* vol.1, Hyderabad, 1929, p.60

9. Najmul Ghani Khan *Tarikh-i-Riyasat-i-Hyderabad, Deccan,* (printed Urdu), Luckhnow, 1930, p.402

10. *Tarikh-i-Rashid-ud-Din Khani* Persian manuscript completed in 1868 SJML 37, p.302, author not given

11. Shah Kamtar *Dastan-i-Nizam Ali Khan, Masanavi* in Deccani Urdu edited by Mir Nizamuddin Ali Khan,Hyderabad, New Delhi, p.71

12. *Op.cit.*, p.46

13. *Op.cit.*, pp.64,65,77

14. Jivan Yar Jung *My Life, Autobiography of Nawab Server-ul-Mulk Bahadur,* London, 1932, p.80

15. Henry Briggs *The Nizam, His History and Relations with the British Government,* vol.1, 1861, reprint, New Delhi, 1988, p.85

16. Sayed Hussain Bilgrami *A Memoir of Sir Salar Jung,* Bombay, 1883, p.46

Rejection of Caste Inequalities by the Sikh Gurus

Surjit Kaur Jolly*

Guru Nanak was a keen observer of the existing social conditions of his times. He reacted quite sharply on the caste system and the degeneration it had brought into the fold of Hindu society. Guru Nanak not only mentions the four *varnas* but also tells us about the duties assigned to them by the society. In *Salok Sahskriti* he says'the way of union with lord is the way of divine knowledge, with the Brahmins the way is through the Vedas. Khatries way is the way of bravery and of the Shudras, the way is the service of the others.[1]

The Brahmins in their private life tried to keep their traditional taboos regarding the preparation of food etc. which was nothing but cheating the masses in the name of superiority of their caste. Guru Nanak strongly denounced the hypocrisy prevalent among caste conscious high caste Hindus in the following lines:

"They seek approval of the Muslim rulers by wearing blue
And they worship the Puranas, succured by the barbarians *(mleccha)* food
And they eat the he goat over which is breathed the foreign word
And they allow no one to enter upon their kitchen square!
They mark off the square, and plaster it with the cow dung.
Let it be defiled last it be defied.
'And this one food be polluted' they cry
But with their impure body, defiled they are,
Their minds are impure, though they cleanse their mouth
Says Nanak Dwell, o man, on the (lords) truth.
For, only if one be pure (of heart) one Attains the Truth.[2]"

This couplet from *Asa Di Var* indicates the hypocrisy, cowardice and false sense of purity possessed by the high caste Hindus. Speaking about the contemporary situation and the role of Kshatriyas it has been stated in Rag Dhansari.

'The Kshatriyas had given up their religion and taken to the foreign tongue. The distinction of'good' and'bad' is obliterated and no one thinks of religion.'[3]

It depicts the loss of moral duty on the part of Kshatriyas which is heroism and defence of the people and the country. Adopting foreign tongue under

*Principal, S. P. M. College, Delhi University, New Delhi

pressure was a symbol of political and cultural subjugation. Vaishya's were considered inferior to the Brahmins and the in the Hindu social structure. The lowest clan among the Hindus was that of the Shudras and the untouchables. It formed a big section of Indian Society (proletariat). They had been assigned a place at the bottom of the social scale. They lived not only under the shadow of contempt but also below the subsistence level of human existence. Their very sight led to the defilement of high caste and they had to announce their movements in various ways. Feeling the pinch of the Shudr's degraded condition in the society Kabir challenged the Brahmins and the superiority of their caste.

> "In the womb of the mother, one knows one's caste.
> It is from the Lord's seed that the whole creation came into being.
> Say o Pandit how did you become a Brahmin born
> Do not lose the merit of thy human birth by calling thyself a high caste.
> If thou are a Brahmin being born of a Brahmin mother
> Then why didn't you chose to be born in some wise difference than the others.
> How are you a Brahmin and I a low caste!
> That I have blood in my veins and you have milk
> Says Kabir 'he alone who contemplates his Lord!
> Is renowned a Brahmin among the men of God."[4]

Likewise in another passage of *Adi Granth* it is asked if Brahmins were different from others why they did not appear in the world by other means than the human birth.

Guru Nanak made a point against caste system on empirical grounds when he points out that laws of nature do not react differently in respect to higher caste men. This empirical evidence is supported and proved by the third Guru Amar Das when he advices against the caste system, 'every one says there are four castes, but it is from God that every one comes. The same is the clay which fashions the whole world, the same clay the potter moulds into vessels of all kinds. The five elements make up the body's form, and who can say who has less of these or more.[5] The Gurus have denied the validity of the caste on the basis of any supposed difference in the fundamental physical constitution of men of the different castes.[6]

Sikh scripture denies that caste is prevalent from the beginning. In the primordial state 'no man of caste or birth, high or low, could be seen 'there was no distinction of colour or caste of the Brahmin and the Kshatriyas.[7] Guru Nanak declares or you ought to see the light within all and not look up for the caste as the caste is of no consequence.[8]

Bhagt Namdev reacts very sharply on the state of affairs, his own caste position and the reaction of almighty God:

> "I come to the temple, O God in a happy mood.
> Whilst in devotion I Nama (Namdev) was caught and asked to get up.
> I belong to a low caste, O Yadav King (lord Krishna)
> Why have I been born in calico printers family
> I took my blanket and turned back, and sat down at the back of the temple.
> As I Nama, utter the praises of Hari (God), the temple of the saints revolves."[9]

By opening the doors of *bhakti* to everybody Sikh Gurus established that 'Vain is the pride of caste, vain is the pride of glory, the lord gives shade to all.'[10] It is declared in the *Adi Granth* that 'who so ever contemplates God, caste or no caste, he is a perfect man of God.'[11] This point has been reinforced by reference to the Hindu fables. Referring to the story of Janak and Sukhadev it says, whosoever is the devotee of God, one must worship him and mind not high or low caste of a devotee; as Sukhadev (a brahmin) stuck to Janaka and Janaka himself anointed his forehead with the dust of nine seers.'[12] Kabir said ' I am a weaver by caste but patient in mind. And so I utter the lord's praise in a state of utter poise.'[13] Bhagat Ravidas is not concerned about the stigma of low caste when he says ' I am a low caste with little honour my birth is low and still'.I am bound to thee with the string of thy love.'[14] It establishes the main principle of Sikhism that caste is no consideration in the realization of the ideal. Men of the so called low caste need not wait to be born again in the next higher caste for the attainment of liberation or spiritual realization. Bhai Gurudas brings out this aspect very clearly when he explains 'As the nature of the utensil has no bearing on the purity of the butter fat similarly the holy men caste have no meaning'.[15]

Sikh Gurus believed in the natural equality of human beings irrespective of their race, religion or birth. Consistence with the universalism it refuses to accredit the caste institution in social ethics. For practical demonstration they associated themselves with the humble and the downtrodden who were discarded as untouchables and unclean. Guru Nanak's two intimate life long companions belonged to two different castes and communities, Mardana, a Muslim Mirasi Bhai Bala a Hindu Khatri. At Saidpur he preferred to stay with Bhai Lalo a carpenter than Malik Bhago. Refusing to dine out at his place Guru Nanak said 'The lowliest of the lowly, the lowest of the low born Nanak seeks their company. The friendship of the great is vain. For where the weak are cared for, there doth thy mercy rain.[16]

By initiating the concept of *'sangat* and *'pangat'* Sikh Gurus did away with all the practical problems of associating with the low caste or the untouchables. In the congregation everybody was supposed to sit together irrespective of caste or creed. From the common kitchen *langar* everybody was supposed to cook and consume the food together. It is said that Guru would not meet people if they refuse to take *langar*. It was to annihilate their ego because of various reasons, at the same time teaching them the principle and strength of equality and unity.

The tenth Guru Gobind Singh declared caste as a taboo in the order of the Khalsa consolidated by him. He says 'true service is the service of these people: I am not inclined to serve others of higher castes; charity will bear fruit, in this and the next world, if given to such worthy people as these.'[17] In Akal Ustat he says 'there is no consideration of caste or membership of *varnas*'.[18]

To join the fraternity of khalsa, worth of human being was given prime position as he had to declare that he had forgotten his past links or caste and has demolished ego of religion or high caste; he had to repeat *'dharma nash','kul nash'* and *'kirti nash'*. The tenth Guru Gobind Singh has established a kind of spiritual equality. After administering baptism to the first five entrants to the khalsa, he himself was initiated in the fraternity by of the same baptism, which was administered to him by the former. Thus, the Guru disciples relationship was also based on equality.[19]

The Rahitnamas (code of conducts or life rules) declare outright rejection of the caste. Bhai Nand Lal the court bard of Guru Gobind Singh reports what Gurus had instructed him 'listen, Nand Lal, I would unite the four varnas in one and lead them to adhere to one God.'[20] When the Brahmins refused to educate the members of this order which included people of the so called lower castes, Sikhs were sent to Kashi, the seat of learning in India at that time, to obtain education and then to serve as educators without the distinctions of caste or birth. The rejection of the caste system is also in corporated in the code of conduct, the Sikh Rahit *maryada* compiled under the warrant of the Shiromani Gurudwara Prabandhak Committee, Amritsar.[21]

It may be concluded that caste system as a whole is rejected in Sikhism. While rejecting it Sikhs mark their departure from the traditional 'objective ethics, or ethical division of the society of the Hindus.' 'The vaccum so created in Sikhism by the outright non acceptance of the traditional institution of *varnadharma* is filled in by laying down equality as the ethical principle of social relations.'[22] The complete equality among all men has been declared by the Sikh Gurus to be the fundamental moral principle required to regulate the social relations. The rejection of castes and the stress on the ideal of universal brotherhood in Sikhism was emphasized to provide equal opportunities to the different sections of the Society to attain the highest possible achievement in this and the other world.

The rise of Sikhism and the teachings of Nanak showed way for a casteless society. It becomes unifying factor for the society. People from various castes came together to form a new order which was against social, political and economic abuse of the time. At least at that time a fraternity developed which stood a safeguard and saviours against the Mughals and Afghans. Part of north India united to challenge the terrorism from extreme North Western frontiers and states.

References

1. Manmohan Singh (tr.) *Adi Granth,* vol. 8, p.4465
2. *Adi Granth,* pp.471-72
3. *Ibid.*, p.663
4. Gopal Singh (tr.) *Adi Granth* vol. I, p.314
5. The three upper castes are termed as twice born as the sacred initiation ceremony is held to be their second birth. The fourth caste is not permitted the sacred initiation and therefore they are not considered to have been born second time in the present life.
6. *Adi Granth,* p.142
7. *Ibid.*, p.1128
8. *Ibid.*, p.349
9. Manmohan Singh (tr.) *Adi Granth,* vol.4, p.1164
10. *Ibid.*, p.83
11. *Ibid.*, p.1178
12. *Ibid.*, p.1309
13. *Ibid.*, p.328
14. *Ibid.*, p.486
15. Bhai Guru Das, *Vars,* stanza 5, var 25
16. Gopal Singh, *op. cit.* vol. I, p.19
17. Guru Gobind Singh *'Hazare Sabad'*
18. Guru Gobind Singh *Akal Ustat*
19. Bhai Nand Lal *Tankhanama*
20. They are called 'Nirmalas' or cleaner pundits of the Khalsa order
21. The *Sikh Rahit Mayaden* pub. S.G.P.C. p.22
22. Avtar Singh *Ethics of the Sikhs,* p.163

Kanhoji Angre – A Curse to the British Sea-borne Trade on the Western Coast (1690-1729)

Kokila Joshi*

So little is known about the life of Kanhoji Angre that number of folk tales are found in Konkan. The *Marathi Vishwakosha* described his native place, Kalose, a village near Pune. Kanhoji Angre's parentage is doubtful. One account says that he was the son of an Arabian Coffer (slave), who had renounced Islam and that for many years he served in the British Company in Bombay as a peon, where they had to bear arms before their masters and walk with their swords laid on their shoulders and their targets flung at their back.'[1] He subsequently fled from Bombay and received a present of Kenery Island and several small gullivats from the Siddis. Another account says that he seemed to have been born in Bombay of a Portuguese Coffer (slave) and a Kenery woman i.e, a Dravidian[2] and that he subsequently escaped to Kenery island and there collected men and ships sufficient to render him the master of the Western coastline.[3] His original surname was Sankpal and as he belonged to Anganwadi close to his village Kalose and may have changed his surname to Angre.[4]

What circumstances, what storm, what chance or accident of war picked the family of Angres from the waterless region of Deccan to and hurled it into the laps of the Arabian sea, neither folklore nor history explains. The earliest reference of an Angre at sea was in the year 1640, but they were not called Angre at that time. In the naval battle between Portuguese and Sultan of Bijapur, in 1640 Kanhoji's father Tukaji seemed to have shown great valour and Portuguese were defeated, bringing the coastline between Chaul and Bombay under the rule of the Sultan of Bijapur. Tukaji was appointed by Shivaji as Samaubat of seaside fort of Suvarnadurg. Thus a naval tradition was established which bound Angre family to the sea and the ships. The name Angre became synonymous with naval might along India's West coast.Sea seemed to have been specially troubled by pirates and the West coast of India had network of pirates, the Sanganias was on of them on the north coast of Kathiawar. There was constant warfare among the Siddis, the Marathas, the Angres and the Sawants.[6] The Portugese advent in India is a story of unbelievable contradictions as they destroyed for all times the traditional feelings and friendliness and hospitality what Konkan has shown to the strangers who came to her ports.

That is the position in which the British found them stooping with the weight of gold in their pockets, but devoid of either crucifix or sword. By this time

*Head of the Department, Dept. of History, R.J. College, Mumbai

the conquerors turned into merchants, at last content to carry on with the profiting of international trading. They were very powerful on sea, as their ships were faster, stronger, heavier and above all better armed than the ships on Indian waters. They compelled all other shipping to acknowledge their authority over the sea. Therefore no ship was permitted to use the waters of the Konkan unless it carried cartoza from the Portuguese Viceroy. They were the unchallenged masters of the Indian Ocean, until the arrival on the scene of Kanhoji Angre, the only ship which could flout the authority of the Portuguese were ships of East India Company.

There were enormous profits to be made from the sale of such things as nickel, lead, mercury, glass beads and mirrors to India and taking away spices, silk, indigo, ivory, muslin, ginger, bees wax and lemon grass to the markets of Europe. But there were larger profits from the sale of slaves and the Company wrote to Kanwar factors 'to supply slaves for export at Rs.15 per head.' They tried to get them more cheaper.[7] As the years passed more factories had to be opened to cope with the increasing volume of trade. Of these Rajapur, Bankote, Karwar and Bombay were in Konkan.

Among the senior Naval Commanders, Kanhoji Angre was responsible to manage the fleet at Suvarnadurg and Gheria with independent command. According to the Portuguese Viceroy Codo-de-Ericiera, the fleet that came to Kanhoji's lot consisted of no more than eight or ten vessels[8] He was by royal command in independent charge of 150 miles of wide open coastline.

The English Company was being knocked about from all sides, but at the same time digging feverishly to entrench themselves in the soil of Konkan. There were two British rival Companies vying with one another jn the campaign of intrigues. These were also the days of piracy on a grand scale. The Malabar pirates had become a terror to the merchants of Surat. Everyone, including the Mughal Emperor was convinced that the pirates were backed by the European companies and many of its servants actually assisted them. The English East India Company had to do a lot of tricky tight rope walking between predatory Angres and the semi-barbarous Siddis.

On the West coast salt is manufactured mainly around Bombay by evaporating seawater captured in saltpans. The whole of Deccan depends upon this salt and English company had pounced upon this vital weakness. Bombay's salt trade with the Maratha country was maintained almost throughout the war in 1698. While some Bombay merchants were returning home with their ships, Maratha grab was set upon them near Padamgad castle and was carried away to their stronghold[9] They demanded ransom worth Rs.20,000, and when they refused to pay, they were imprisoned and were barbarously treated. On their signing bond for Rs.2000 all were released, except two English men, kept as hostages. Six Marathas accompanied the merchant to Bombay to receive the promised money. On hearing the outrage, Bombay Government arrested the Maratha agents and informed that they would be released only if British hostages were released. The British reacted to this incident by placing an embargo on all ships belonging to Bombay, forbidding them to carry salt to any place along the coast, until full assurance from the Subedars made that such abuses should not be done to our people in future.

Kanhoji Angre had shown tactical wisdom beyond his years of experience and had scrupulously avoided major showdown with Portuguese or British. He learnt to look at warfare with far more detachment and realized that success in the battlefield was not merely a matter of blind courage, that scrupulous avoidance of unnecessary risks was just as important as any requirements of tactics[10] During Maratha war of independence (1689-1707) they fought in order to reconquer their forts and territories and also for their livelihood. Kanhoji made prizes of vessels belonging to all nations, plundered most of the towns along the coast from Bombay to Travancore and occupied forts like Suvarnadurg, Kolaba and Vijaydurg.

The Court of Directors instructed Governor Gayor to make Bombay centre of their trade and the riding place of their shipping[11] But during Maratha Mughal wars of late 17th century Companie's factories faced constant danger of being plundered causing loss to their trade. In Feb 1695 Surat Council wrote, 'the roads are much infected by Raja Ram's troops who have plundered Dungaon and other adjacent town in the province of Khandesh, Aurangabad, Agra and Kandahar became hazardous to travelers. It led to scarcity of commodity, little less than famine in most parts of this great kingdom, it will be difficult carrying on the cloth trade.'[12] There was apprehension of Raja assaulting Surat and sack it, which had put Surat's trade to stop for which arms and ammunition and 20 topasses[13] for defence of factory was sent. There were reports of daily interruptions in their commercial activities'[14]

Surat Council wrote again in April 1695 'no sooner were the ships gone but the town was in great confusion at the approach of some of Shivaji's (Marathas) troops near Nandurbar. Our Governor put the town in the best picture of defence he could; Dutch, French and we did the same to our several factories. Trade is wholly at a stand. We had no small trouble to send Your Honor's goods with us to Swally, we shall continuously be exposed to such alarms.'[15] 'At Karwar we expected a large quantity of pepper about this time; but by our late letters from thence we are informed that Shivaji (Kanhoji) has overrun all the Raja's country, plundering and burning all before him, but now we hear again that the business is like to be made up with money; if so, we may have a quantity of pepper there.'[16]

The problem of piracy in the west coast added further checks for the growth of Bombay trade. The Bombay Council's letter in 1691 says 'trade was generally hampered by the large number of pirates along the coast, who were alleged to be the Angres. The British Government issued proclamation against all pirates, but it had very little effect, for between 22nd March to 30th Oct 1791, at least seven serious outrages upon the high seas were reported by the Surat Council to the Court of Directors[17].

Kanhoji Angre was appointed by Rajaram's Admiral of the Maratha fleet in 1698. His ships crept along the coast, plundering every vessel and sailing up every creek to sack the undefended towns. Shivaji had guarded every creek with a fort and these fell into Angre's hands. The fleets of Angre consisted of fast sailing vessels of small weight and rowing boats or 40 to 50 boats manned by desperate men. From the creeks in which their fleet lay these men of the Konkan pounced upon their prey. They would smother their victims and fire into her rigging until they succeed in disabling her whereupon the rowing boat closed in and the crew, handed with swords boarded her from all sides.'[18]

Both Kanhoji Angre and Portuguese took advantage of the weakness of the state of Bombay. Company wrote letters of complaints to both Rajaram and Tarabai, but the affairs were so complicated that they could not expect better treatment. Bombay government did not want to be hostile to them, but finding danger of their attacks and trade affected everyday, they asked permission of the Home authorities to resist aggressors by force of arms.

Kanhoji did not care who the ruler or whose property it was, as plunder was his profession and pursued the same policy on the sea. In 1699 Charles Perris, the Captain of English ship 'thankful' was attacked and the Captain gave its interesting account, 'in sight of Batticola saw 12 sails of Kanhoji, grabs and boats which seven in the morning came to us. One boat hailed us; we told them we were of Bombay. He went to the rest and fired at us -we fired at them; the fight lasted till one in the afternoon at which time they repeated it about half an hour and then it was calm. They sounded their trumpet and came on again, at which time I called them again and would not fire a gun at them, send one boat on board, then it could take her to fight again. They came and demanded Rs 2000, without which they would take the ship. I told them, if they want war, we were ready to fight again, and would not fire a gun at them, before they came on board. They went with this answer to their Admiral and came again and asked Rs 100 and some rice. I told them, I would give nothing. They rowed a little towards us and then turned and went away.'[19] Council of Surat informed, Bombay's shipping merchantmen had to be convoyed for Kanhoji had grown strong and independent, scare any boat passing to and fro from the island without convoy.[20]

By the beginning of the 18th century, the English Company dispatched their agents to establish factories and open trade with India under the Emperor's *farman*. The attacks of Kanhoji caused so much alarm that the factors failed to get indigo. The Marathas began to think that the Konkan and its coastal water belonged to them. Thus, Kanhoji introduced *dastak* or permit system for any foreign ship plying along their coast and he had already begun to offer *dastak* to all sea going ships in return for protection from pirates and other coastal powers. Ships without *dastak* would be seized and held for ransom. The Portuguese and Angres claimed ownership of the Konkan waters and the British would not stand any interference from either.

There had been no open hostilities between Kanhoji Angre and the British Company after 1698 assurance by the latter. Company's men had supported the Siddis the enemy of Kanhoji Angre 'in order to use the Siddis as a foil to Angre'.[21] Within three years there was hardening of the British attitude towards him which later broke into a declaration of war. The restrictions imposed on coastal trading ships had begun to cut into the Companie's profits and the growing naval power of Angres had disturbed their balance of trade.

In 1702 Kanhoji happened to seize a merchant ship at Calicut, which had six Englishmen on the board. The vessel was private one and the Englishmen had merely taken passage on it. British always treated such ship as their own and thus granted all treaty privileges and facilities that the Company's own ships might be entitled to. The Bombay Council wrote a sharp letter to Kanhoji asking for the immediate release of the ship. He replied, 'He would give cause to remember his name'. The captured Englishmen were released after the payment of ransom.

In 1703 Kanhoji seized a Dutch warship of 30 guns and at this time English and Dutch were allies. There was little friendship between the Dutch and English and the perpetual enmity between the two was expressed at Anjengo at Malabar Coast. They had no reason to be angry when Kanhoji had seized the Dutch ship, but British Company was waiting for a chance to teach him a lesson. In Sept 1703, there came a ship loaded with cargo from Aden on the Bombay shore. It was registered in Rajapur and carried Kanhoji's *dastak*. The Bombay Council decided to detain both the ship and the passengers but did not clarify the condition for its release. The British ship Captains also attacked Spanish and French ships including the ship of the Mughal emperor. Kanhoji allowed this open net of piracy on the part of the British merchants to go unheeded.

Reports of the movement of Kanhoji' s fleet kept Bombay on an alert day and night and made them to protect their shipping and prevent surprise landing on the island. In Dec 1702, a betel nut ship under Captain Doughty was set upon by eight Maratha grabs and gullivats near Kolaba and took its crew and Captain as prisoners. A few days later Kanhoji appeared with his fleet near Versova and the Deputy Governor wrote to him demanding immediate release of the prisoners, boat and cargo. He also sent cruise 'between Versova and Malabar hill so as to keep a good watch upon the movement of Kanhoji Angre. The order was not to assault Kanhoji, but to prevent him from attacking or capturing vessels bound to Bombay[22] Kanhoji demanded Rs 5000 ransom. Thus British decided to meet force by force; but for this island fleet was not strong enough[23] Some more boats and *machuvas* were then armed and few ships were also built. Kanhoji took good care not to expose himself to the danger of risky battles but continued his trade of piracy. He was now independent of Maratha government and acted on his own initiative.

Kanhoji Angre's constant loot embittered the British officers. A letter to the Council of Surat says, 'the experience we had of perfidious heathen Kanhoji Angre hath given us sufficient cause to be cautious, how we trust him or any of his caste, and shall use our utmost endeavors to prevent his evil designs against this island and its inhabitants. Kanhoji lies now in his den at Suvarnadurg castle.'[24] Kanhoji was developing into the pest of the sea, as the Portuguese acquired Elephanta and the Angres got Konnery which alarmed Bombay as they felt this place would be used for more attacks and looting by Marathas. The British Deputy Governor strongly rebuked for pretending to be friend and demanded delivery of vessels. Kanhoji said that in future he would make no depredations and perform all his promises.'[25]

The new Governor of Bombay Sir John Gayer warned Kanhoji when he seized the ships of the merchants trading in Bombay. It caused great loss to the island and thus he resolved to follow a definite policy with regard to him. They wanted to send Mr. Reynold to go to Kanhoji, 'clearly telling him that he cannot be permitted searching, molesting or seizing grabs or boats or other vessels from any harbour, port, place and whatsoever the nation may have bringing provision like timber or merchandise to Bombay, Mahim or other places from whence, they come without breach of that friendship which they had with Shivaji and all other Captains of the Maratha navy, said Mr. W. Reynold, is not upon any account whatsoever by words or otherwise to threaten or entertain any design of hostilities against him, but respectfully taking leave, come away.'[26] The government had made up their mind that if Kanhoji refused to accept the terms, they wou1d surprise him and destroy his fleet.

The British company treated Kanhoji as an independent naval commander of Chhatrapati, but in their dealings with him he was treated as Chhatrapati's officer. As a pirate, of course he could not be tolerated. Kanhoji replied to the British that the Marathas' were the friends of English but the latter did not respond like that. While all the Portuguese ports were open to Marathas and as they lived by their swords they would seize the boats of Mughals or other Europeans upto the Malabar coast, unless they carried Kanhoji's pass.[27]

During the civil war with Tarabai, Shahu had asked the British Company at Bombay to supply powder, shots, fire lances, soldiers and some money. But the Governor sent diplomatic reply 'there has been for many years a friendly alliance preserved between Shivaji and English Company, until Kanhoji Angre, without legal authority, took upon to violate these ancient articles by robbing ships and vessels belonging to the inhabitants under the said powerful Company with the colours and passports permitted by our magnificent and great Queen, which hitherto has not been punished, believing Kanhoji as vassel to the Raja. When the Company did not receive any reply from Tarabai about Kanhoji's misrule, they decided to blow up and destroy his forts along the seacoast. The Desais of Kalyan had sent the Governor a word that Shahu was the true Raja and lord of the country who would give justice in this regard[28] Shahu did not receive any help as no definite reply was given for punishment to Kanhoji.

In 1706 Kanhoji's men attacked and captured the Company's ship 'Monsoon' off Karwar but then released it at his port Gheria when he faced their attacks. In 1707 Kanhoji's ship attacked and sank British Company's ship 'Frigate' and in 1710 his ship had two days long battle with Company's ship 'Godolphin' near Bombay. In 1710, Company complained to the Directors that Kanhoji 'could take any ship, except the largest European ships, along the coast from Surat to Dabhol, he takes all private merchants shipments. After 1710 some peace was found between Kanhoji and the British Company. But in no time the peace was disturbed by Kanhoji when he attacked the British Captain Peacock in Somers and Captain Collet in Grantham. He continued to harass the British trade at Bombay.

In 1712 Kanhoji captured two more British Company's ships, one was the Governor's own armed 'Yatch' and the other ship was 'Ketch Anne' belonged to Company's chief factors at Karwar. Both these ships were taken after stiff fight near Vengurla, during which their armed escort 'Defiance' had been put to flight. Kanhoji attacked two more ships of the Company within a month of the attack on British ships. The British Council was alarmed by Kanhoji' s boldness and thus the Viceroy proposed joint attack on Kanhoji with the help of Portuguese and Siddis. In 1713 the British Company and Kanhoji signed a treaty of friendship. Treaty of Kolaba was signed between Kanhoji Angre and British Company. It was more like a treaty of non -belligerence and not a treaty of friendship. Kanhoji promised that he would not attack any ships entering between Mahim and Khandevi and he would allow British merchant in free trade in his ports and in returns Kanhoji was also granted liberty in British ports to buy and sell merchandise by paying the usual custom dues. Kanhoji obtained ten sea side ports and sixteen land forts and his annual income was thirty-six lakh rupees. He was confirmed with the authority of *Sarkhail.* The whole of Konkan, from Bombay to Goa with exception of three small strips, was formally recognized under his command.

In Dec 1715, Charles Boone became the Governor of Bombay. He received petitions from the people of Bombay complaining 'of heavy oppression and injuries they had received from Kanhoji the pirate, who was then at Kolaba and island of Konnery with strong castle of Gheria'.[29] The continuous piracies of Kanhoji and other Europeans caused so much alarm to the Court of Directors that they wanted to send an expedition against them. Thus, in Feb 1721, Commodore Mathew sailed with a Squadron from Spited and arrived in Bombay in Sept 1721.

Downing who had accompanied Governor Boone to Bombay gives an account of this expedition. In 1716 Kanhoji seized a ship within full sight of Bombay harbour, which had English flag, but it belonged to an Indian merchant. Early in 1717, he followed this up by capturing three more Indian ships, which did not carry his *dastaks* and it tried to pass them off as the Company's ships by using English flag. It led to an exchange of sharp letters between Governor Boone and Kanhoji. The Company insisted that any ship, which carried cargo belonging to the Council of Bombay or to any other of the Company's Council in India was exempted from taking *destak*-from Kanhoji. Thus, he retorted that only such ships were entitled to exemption, which actually belonged to the Company.

Governor Boone in 1716 sent off his ships to attack Vengurla, which still had a small Dutch Factory. Governor Boone may have sent it to oust Dutch from there or may have been sent to subdue Sawants of Wadi. British ships 'Fame', 'Britania' and 'Revenge' sailed out for their mission of destruction. For two whole days they bombarded Vengurla from different directions. Due to differences of policy between the Squadron leader and the Commander of Infantry, the ships returned to Bombay without serving any purpose. After the Vengurla 'fiasco, Governor Boone, sacked Mr. Hemilton, as Commander- in chief of Company's fleet. In September the Squadron sailed for Karwar to defeat its Raja and cleverly took promise of help from the Portuguese of Goa so that his forces could get supplies from Goa, to Karwar. Once again the expedition completely failed due to indiscipline and double-dealings of his officers.

The capture of the four Indian ships by Kanhoji in 1716 which the British Company had been passing off as English ships, once again led to exchange of letters between the British Company and Kanhoji. Towards the end of 1716 Kanhoji attacked another ship 'Success', which belonged to the Company's broker at Surat, Gordhan Das. The Company insisted that it was their ship therefore should be exempted from Kanhoji's *dastak.* Governor Boone would not risk war but contented by sending stiff protest to Kanhoji and advised Gordhan Das to get the release of his ship by negotiation. British messenger proved to be an obstacle in the settlement of the issue. During the process of the negotiation, news reached Bombay that another ship 'Robert' carrying Englishmen as passengers was seized by Kanhoji's men. Before the matter could be solved Kanhoji had forcibly took over one of the Company's boats into Kolaba and from it removed some pieces of timber.

The removal of timber gave the British Council a cause for anger more than the capture of the ships and its English passengers. The timber actually belonged to the Company but they were in no mood to risk the war with Kanhoji. They wrote letter to him demanding the release of the seized ship and their English passengers but Kanhoji flatly declined to release either ships or the passengers, as the ships belonged to the Indian merchants and not to the Company. He made the entire episode as a prank and asked the Governor not to spoil their friendship on such trivial issue. Rama Kamathi was deputed to Kanhoji for the release of British ships and passengers, but even he failed in the mission. The matter was further complicated when Kanhoji captured another English ship 'Otter' belonged to the Bengal Council.

Kanhoji Angre made it clear that he would not molest the ships those genuinely belong to the British Company. But if they will freight without a pass, they could be captured. They adopted such practice to freight 50 to 100 ships of Surat merchants which will deprive him of his legitimate *dastak* fees and custom dues. This had encouraged the ship owners to flout the Maratha domination of the coast. Even the British used the practice of issuing *dastaks* and seizing ships which did not bear their *dastaks* Governor Boone was in no mood to give thought to the contemporary maritime practice. Thus, on 5th April 1718 the Bombay Council issued secret orders to their fighting ships to capture or sink Kanhoji' s ships if they happened to run into them. Thus ship 'Shibar' belonged to Kanhoji's squandrom at Alibag was captured by the British ship and it was taken to Bombay. The seizure of one of his naval boat is a flagrant violation of the treaty between him and the British Company. He wrote to the Company, 'our friendship is over, and from this day forward, what God gives, I shall take.'[30] Boone ordered his naval staff to sink or seize Kanhoji's ships.

The attack on Gheria was much more than an attempt of capturing it as they designed to capture it at a single stroke as large part of Kanhoji' s ships were huddled up in its monsoon anchorage. Governor Boone bribed Kanhoji's advisor, Manuel de Castro who knew everything about Kanhoji' s fleets and Gheria was a natural target, which had the largest number of ships at anchor situated far from Satara and Kolaba who could give them no help. It was a surprise attack and merciless shelling went on for two days. But the original plan of Gheria expedition misfired forcing British Commander to return back to Bombay. The British then attacked Khanderi another strong hold of Kanhoji in November 1718. The .defence of Khanderi was nothing sort of a brilliant tactical victory, but Company's poor military reputation was a chief casualty.

By the beginning of 1720's the peace talk between British and Kanhoji failed as war resumed. Kanhoji captured some Mughal ships on 14th May 1720 off Surat. The Governor of Surat Ismail Khan separately appealed Bombay to plan a joint attack on Kanhoji with the help of Portuguese. But Governor Boone did not respond and felt that the situation demanded a concerted effort. He suggested to Mughal Subedar to keep patrol boat to guard Surat coast and with their Emperor's mediation they could take Siddi's help and assist the British to attack Kanhoji by land and sea. William Brown, the Commander of British Squadron failed to bend or break Kanhoji. British no doubt were in a position to invade any of a dozen places along the coast, if once they succeed in capturing Kanhoji's main fort. He found it impossible to maintain a permanent garrission, strong enough to repel a major British naval attack. He was hostile to his southern neighbour, the powerful Sawant of Wadi who had begun to come into open.

Kanhoji's campaign of capturing English ships continued relentlessly, but he was careful of capturing ships which did not bear his *dastaks*. He took care of not interfering in Portuguese shipping. The Siddis had become friendlier than in the past, and they had assisted him in his negotiations for the return of Mughal ships to the Viceroy of Surat. The task of Bombay's dealings with Kanhoji was more stirring, when they attacked Kanhoji's ship at Varli and they carried one of them to Bombay. He retorted by capturing Bombay's ship in 1728 as well as attacked another British ship namely 'King William' commanded by Mc Neule, who tried to escape fruitlessly and paid Rs 300 ransom to Kanhoji. In the midst of British attack on his stronghold Khanderi, Kanhoji died in 1729.

Although the British trade was disturbed in the West Coast by the repeated attempt of Kanhojis to seize merchant ships, the Company did not face any financial loss. Whenever the plan to defend British controlled harbours were put forward, they met the expenses by obtaining 'contributions' from the native merchants of Bombay and Surat. In these years whenever British Company suffered a trading loss, it was always made up by boosting up the port dues or custom fees or even by levying special taxes. So that jn the last analysis such losses were paid up by the Indian merchants.

References

1. Edward, S.M. *Gazetteer of Bombay City and Island*, vol. 2, Printed at Government Press, p. 82
2. *Ibid.*, p. 83
3. Downing, C. *A Compendius History of Indian Wars*-1737. Among Angre's Chief Captain was Janius Plantain, son of a pirate Avery. He had 6008, Hindu sepoys and two kolis from Bombay. *Bombay Gazetteers* vol., 1, p. 87
4. Lokshastri Joshi (Ed.) *Maratha Vishwakosh* vol. 1, Marathi Rajya Sanskriti Mandal, Mumbai, 1976, p.76
5. Malgaonkar Manohar *Kanhoji* Angre, the *Maratha Admiral*, Asia pub., Pune, 1959, p.12
6. Desai, W.C. *Bombay and the Marathas*, Munshiram Pub., Delhi, 1970, p.49
7. Sarkar. J. N. *House of Shivaji*, Orient Lingmens, Calcutta, 1919, p.29. This letter goes to say 'these pair of dwarfs (man and woman) are to be sent home to his Majesty'.
8. *Op.cit.*, 1959, p.61
9. *Maharashtra Archives* Factory Records, *India Office*, vol. 16, Born Con dated 19-1-1699
10. *Op. cit.*, 1970, p. 65
11. *Maharashtra Archives* Letter Books, India Office, Ms vol. 9, dated 26-9-1693
12. *Maharashtra Archives* Official Correspondence, India Office, Ms.5969 to the Court of Directors
13. Eurasian soldiers; the term is perhaps the corruption of 'topchi' which means gunner It may mean 'topiwala', batman
14. *Maharashtra Archives* Official Correspondence 6003 to the Directors dated 28-3-.1695
15. *Ibid.*, 6231, Surat to the Directors dated 16-9-1696
16. *Ibid.*, 6393, Bombay to Directors dated 28-4-697
17. Edward.S.N. *Rise of Bombay*, Government Press, Pune, 1908. Surat Council to the Court of Directors dated Jan 12, 1698, p.48
18. *Maharashtra Archives* Selection from state papers 1881, 7
19. *Maharashtra Archives Official Correspondence* 6473 dated 6-12-1697, Bombay to the Directors
20. *Maharashtra Archives Official Correspondence* 6542 dated 10-4-1697
21. *Op.cit.*, 1959, p.96
22. *Maharashtra Archives Bombay Consultations of the Council*, India Office
23. *Maharashtra Archives* Bombay letters from Factory Records, India Office Ms.vol18 dated 11-3-1703
24. *Maharashtra Archives* Factory Records, India Office dated 10-9-1703
25. *Ibid.*, vol 18, Bombay letters dated 15-1-1704
26. *Maharashtra Archives* Bombay Public Proceedings; India Office Ms. vol 2 dated 24-11-1704
27. *Ibid.*, dated 27-.1-1708
28. *Ibid.*, vol. 3, Castle dated 29-1-1708
29. *Op. cit.*, vol. 2, p.86
30. *Op. cit.*, 1959, p.196

The ASI'S Report on Ayodhya

Irfan Habib*

The Archaeological Survey of India's report on its Ayodhya excavations, submitted to the Special Branch of the High Court has been widely acclaimed by the RSS and VHP spokesmen for giving the official stamp of approval to their claims of the previous existence of a temple at the Babri Masjid site. This is, indeed, true though it is another matter that the hand that wields the official stamp is controlled by the very same people who do the applauding. It is another matter still, whether what the ASI says in its report is true.

An important handicap to the ASI in the present case has been that the entire excavations were constantly watched by a team of archaeologists independent of ASI. This was because of the High Court's orders. The result is that whereas in its ordinary excavations the ASI works totally in private, without any monitoring eye, it has been otherwise in the case of its Ayodhya excavations. Everything that was dug up, and how it was dug up, and recorded, was seen and often verified by the litigants' nominees. The result is that one can check up on what the ASI says, it found there and the inferences it has drawn from them. For really the first time the ASI's methods and integrity have been put to a public test.

How, then, has it fared in this public test? The ASI claims that the High Court asked it to determine 'whether there was any temple/ structure which was demolished and mosque was constructed on the disputed site.' The ASI, however, proceeds in its report as if the word ' whether' was not used at all by the court, and its task was simply to prove that a temple had, indeed, existed at the site- not only just a temple, but a very grand one. The first thing it has therefore done is to brush aside altogether any evidence that could go against the presence of a temple.

First, take the total omission of any examination of animal bones. It is casually admitted in the Summary of Results on page 270 that 'animal bones have been recovered from various levels of different periods.' But in the main Report there is no examination and description of the animal bones at all: no identification of the species of animals (mostly, apparently, sheep and goat), and no tabulation by trench and level of the bones, especially those with cut-marks (attesting to meat consumption on the spot). The motive is obvious: their presence everywhere at all (not just 'various') levels is destructive of any thesis of there having been any temple at the site previous to the mosque. Animals are surely not eaten and their

*Former Professor of History Aligarh Muslim University, Aligarh.
The paper was distributed in a press conference at New Delhi.

bones deposited in a temple.

Bones are organic material and can also be carbon-dated. It is strange, then, that the bones at the Babri Masjid site were not carbon-dated, so that their dates could have definitely settled the issue of the possibility of the temple at the site during the period they were deposited.

Another important factor negativing the presence of the temple is the finding of medieval ('Muslim') glazed ware beneath all the floor levels, including the floor attributed to the temple by the ASI. Yet when some of these are listed (p.108 onwards), there is no reference to the actual level where they were found. Nor is there any tabulation level-wise of glazed ware fragments. The reason again is obvious enough. Such tabulation was bound to show the presence of glazed ware below the imagined 'temple floor', and thus would have exposed the fiction.

While the ASI has thus brushed under the carpet all the evidence directly contradicting the temple theory, it has gone on to invent the evidence for what is now called a ' Massive Structure below the Disputed Structure'. When one sits down to examine the theory closely, one immediately finds how fantastic it is.

Four floors have been discovered; all of them have lime-mortar bonding, a sure sign of sultanate and post-Sultanate construction. It is obvious from the presence of lime-mortar in the floor and attached walls that Floor 4, the lowest floor, belongs to the Sultanate period. A mihrab having been found in an attached wall the Floor 4, the lowest floor, belongs to the Sultante period. A *mihrab* having been found in an attached wall (ignored in the Report), it is certain, that it belongs to a pre-Mughal open (*qanati*) mosque or *idgah*. In order to tide over this difficulty and make the early mosque-floor into a temple floor, the Report creates a period unknown to history- period Vi, Medieval-Sultanate Level'- which it proceeds to place in ' the eleventh-twelfth century' (p.40). Our ASI is so knowledgeable these days that it does not know that the Delhi Sultanate itself was established in 1206, i.e., in the thirteenth century, to which alone the lime-mortar floor could have belonged at the earliest. There was no question of its having been used in the 11th and the 12th centuries (the Gahadavala period). It is further to be noted that in this supposedly 'huge structure' (of a temple) only four so-called 'pillar-bases' have been found; and the Report concedes ruefully that the construction of the temple must have been incomplete ('short-lived') (Report, p.269). All the remaining 46 'pillar-bases' belong, therefore, to the period after 1200. they contain not only mud bonding but also lime mortar and thus follow Muslim methods of construction. Are we, then, to suppose, following the ASI's inferences, that the great temple was built under Muslim rulers, the Delhi Sultans and the Sharqi rulers of Jaunpur?

The '50 pillar bases' are, the only argument left for a temple, even if 46 of these have to be dated to the Sultanate times. These are curious 'pillar bases', indeed, in that they have no association anywhere with any pillar! They generally comprise calcrete stones resting on loose or mud-bonded brickbats. How such a 'base' could ever carry a stone or brick pillar that has to sustain a masonry roofing strains one's credulity. Despite the claims and fancy drawings (figures 23, 23A and 23 following p.42) these are not actually in alignment. The ASI report omits the elementary requirement of detailed grid-plans for a simple reason: these can be checked for the trenches are still not closed, by the Court's orders. Not only are they badly aligned, if aligned at all, these 'pillar bases' are sealed by, or they themselves pierce, either Floor 3 or Floor 2 of the Mosque, as already shown by ASI's own earlier reports. It would have been a shaky structure indeed, which was held up by pillars resting on heaps of brickbats at different levels!

The fact is that these are neither pillar bases nor 'structural bases' (the description in ASI's interim report of work upto 24 April). To my friend Dr. Ashok Dutta of Kolkata, an experienced archaeologist, who himself watched these excavations, I owe the most satisfactory explanation. They are remains of brickbats put into hollows of ground in order to make it level. Calcrete stones were put at the top to press them into place, and then the floor was laid out. As time passed and the mosque had to be refloored, brickbats were again put in to close holes and depressions in the floor in order to lay out a new one. That is why they are all over the place and under practically all the floors, and so at different levels. The ASI simply ignored those heaps which its team considered too far out of 'alignment' for their purposes. Otherwise, they could well have marked a hundred or more of such heaps. But they sustained no pillars, they only provided level ground for mosque flooring.

I end with another absurdity. Much is made out of the 'Circular Shrine' (Report, pp.70-71), with fanciful drawings (Fig. 24 and 24 A). Comparisons with other circular Hindu shrines are made (Figs. 18) though not, of course, with any Muslim circular domed buildings! When a careful reader looks at the Plan of the Circular Shrine on Fig. 17, thankfully drawn to scale, its total diameter (inclusive of the thick wall) is found to be just 180 cms or less than 6 feet! Moreover, the wall does not even make quarter of a circle, so that even this smallest of 'circular shrines' is just a piece of the ASI's own imagination.

The ASI's Report on Ayodhya is no credit to its authors. It may serve its short-term purpose in giving the saffron forces something to exult over. But in so doing it has done immense harm to the good repute and credibility of what was once a great organisation, the Archaeological Survey of India.

Imagining Second Mosque at Ayodhya — A Critique of Irfan Habib's 'The ASI Report on Ayodhya'

S.P. Gupta*

Backdrop

Shifting Stands and the Great Somersault: from 'Nothing Found in Excavations' to Remains of Two Mosques Found in Excavations!

On 10th and 16th June 2003, Irfan Habib told to the press (*Hindu* and *Asian Age 11th June; Times of India* 17th June) that 'nothing has been found in the excavations' and the whole exercise has been an utter waste of time and energy of the ASI. It was flashed all over the world through the mass media. Recently, however, the very same people have shifted their stand and took a somersault since the Excavation Report entitled *Ayodhya 2002-2003*, has been made public on 25th August 2003, informing the world that there were indeed hundreds of objects and remains of various buildings immediately below the disputed structure. So much so that the foundation walls of the Disputed Structure or the Baburi Mosque have been found directly overlying the walls of a temple of the North Indian Style, called 'Nāgar Style', implying thereby that the so-called 'Baburi Mosque' was built after destroying a pre-existing temple at this site and directly over the ruins of the temple.

The ASI Report is in two volumes. The 1st volume has the text running in 308 pages, fully illustrated with dozens of charts, tables and line-drawings of Plans and Sections of the excavated remains. While the 2nd has 237 photographs of structural remains and movable antiquities. In the light of this revelation these scholars accepted the discovery of material remains unearthed at Ramajanmabhumi, Ayodhya, though reluctantly and with riders, as may be seen from a write-up of Irfan Habib circulated in the form of xeroxed copies and published in this issue of *History Today*.

Thus, since the findings have gone against the Masjid protagonists, they have started a malicious campaign against the ASI Report by imagining a mosque of the Sultanate Period which had never existed at Janmabhumi; the only mosque like structure 'meant for Angles to descend on' according to a Persian inscription found here earlier, that existed at the site was the so-called 'Baburi Mosque' of the 16th century. Moreover, very cleverly Habib avoided to name the Sultan who may have built this 'imagined mosque', afterall the Sultans ruled for more than 300 years and they were so many of them. Is this history or cat-and-bull story?

*Chairman, Indian Archaeological Society, New Delhi

In any case, what is being attempted by Irfan Habib has not been supported, backed and substantiated by any source of history, literature, tradition, epigraphy, numismatics, manuscripts, *farmāns, sanads, nishāns,* Muslim and Hindu alike. So much so that even the grand-daughter of Aurangzeb, who wrote the famous book *Safiha-i-Chahal-Nasaih Bahādur Shāhī* in the late 17th century, has not mentioned any sultanate period mosque at all, she talks only of the so-called 'Baburi Mosque'. In fact, we will be happy to be proven wrong if any scholar in India or abroad can give us proof of the existence of a Sultanate Period Mosque at Ramjanmabhumi; it is a very serious matter and opinions of motivated historians can not be taken as proof. It is sheer ploy.

1.The animal bones valid in temple context or mosque context? The ritual of animal sacrifice in temples or in mosques?

The first point raised by Irfan Habib concerns the presence of animal bones in different excavated levels which have yielded debris from outside to raise floors. Though the animal species to which they belonged have not yet been identified by zoologists, Irfan Habib takes them as sheep and goat. He then says, 'Animals are surely not eaten and their bones deposited in a temple' in order to prove that there could never be a temple at the Ramajanmabhumi site. It is a peculiar argument since no bone has been found in the primary context of the temple.

Two things. First, animal sacrifice is a common feature in most of the temples, for example, the Bimala Devi shrine in the Jagannath Temple, Puri, the Kali Temple of Kolkata, the Kamakhya Temple of Guwahati, the Masuria Temple of Allahabad and practically all the temples of Uttaranchal. These are only a few examples of those temples where goat and sheep have been regularly sacrificed and their meat eaten by the devotees for hundreds of years. Therefore, if the bones of sheep and goats are found in the *debri* brought from outside to the temples at Ramajanmabhumi what is surprising in it? It may be noted that not a single animal bone has been found from within the temples. Even the Circular Shrine has not yielded a single piece of animal bone. Where is then the question of 'deposited in a temple'? It is sheer twisting the archaeological evidence intentionally and with a purpose, sinister as it is. On the contrary, is there any evidence of animal sacrifice in mosques? Do the Muslims eat animal flesh in mosques and then deposit the bones in mosques? Does the presence of goat and sheep bones in the debris of a temple, or even within a temple, will automatically mean that it was a mosque and not a temple? The answers of all these questions will be just 'No'.

2. The use of lime mortar in india: Sultanate or pre-Sultanate? 5000 years of history of the use of lime mortar in india for bonding, flooring and plastering stone and brick structures

Second point. Habib says, 'four floors have been discovered; all of them have lime-mortar bonding, a *sure sign of Sultanate and post-Sultanate construction*', 'the presence of lime-mortar in the floor and attached walls' would show 'floor 4, the lowest floor, belongs to Sultanate period.' It is utter falsehood.

This statement apparently means that the lime-mortar (a) used as bonding material, (b) used in flooring, and (c) used as plaster on walls and floors came to India with the Sultans of Delhi who came from Ghazni in Afghanistan and who established their regular rule in Mehrauli area in 1206 A.D. In other words, the Hindus did not know the technique of producing lime from *kankar* and use it with the admixture of coarse materials like sand in their constructions, and the Muslims, when they came to Delhi, taught them the technique of exacting lime from *kankar* and also its use for preparing mortar for joining bricks and stones and plastering walls. It only betrays utter ignorance of the history of science and technology of ancient India on the part of Irfan Habib, who is, in any case, only a scholar of economic history of medieval India. I, therefore, won't greatly blame him for this kind of his ignorance but I do blame him for presenting false history of India to the nation.

The massive use of lime-mortar, let it be noted, is

attested to in the Harappan cities of the third millennium B.C. Later on it is found used in the 3rd century B.C. at Bhir Mound, Taxila, Pakistan. In the 2nd century B.C., i.e., at least 1500 years before the coming of Delhi Sultans, the builders of the famous dome of the Buddhist Stupa at Sanchi had made use of it. The dome has thick lime plaster, found by Sir John Marshall, and can still be seen *in situ*. Percy Brown has quoted the archaeological evidence of the use of lime mortar at Besanagar (Vidisha) as recorded by Alexander Cunningham: 'portions of the foundations consisted of bricks cemented together by a well-made grade of lime mortar - bricks were grooved to hold the lime mortar.' That the lime-mortar was used during the Kushana Period also (1st century A.D.-3rd century A.D.) for example at Mathura, has been recorded by its excavator, Shri M.C. Joshi, former Director General, Archaeological Survey of India. At Sirkap in Taxila also *bajari*-lime mortar was used during this period as has been recorded by the excavators, including Sir John Marshall and recently by Pakistani archaeologists who reported it in *Pakistan Archaeology,* Vol.VI. At Kaushambi in Uttar Pradesh the lime mortar had high percentage of lime as the chemical analysis has undoubtedly shown. It is common knowledge that lime-mortar was extensively used in bonding bricks, in plastering walls and in finishing floors during the Gupta Period (400 A.D.-600 A.D.) at Nalanda, Aphsad and many other places in Bihar.

From the 7th to the 10th century Nalanda used the lime mortar in the ratio of 3:2 (lime+sand). Jars with dried up mortar and a cell used as cistern to make the mortar have been found at Nalanda. At Karvan, District Vadodara, Gujarat two kinds of lime mortar were used in the Gupta buildings, one with higher content of lime and the other lower. At Bhitari, District Gazipur, in Uttar Pradesh the lime and sand ratio in the mortar was 6:1. The red colour of the mortar and plaster has been due to the use of ferruginous *kankar* in the making of the lime. Lime mortar and surkhī with lime were used at Bangarh also during the Gupta period. It was used extensively in the temple construction of Nara Nath in Kashmir, and Purana Qila, Delhi, both of the 8th - 9th century. In the 10th century temple of Lingraj at Bhubaneswar lime-mortar was used extensively. Lime mortar was also used in the Kanchipuram temple of the same period. Lime mortar was also used in the Arthuna Temple of Rajasthan. At Sarnath it was used during the rule of the Gahadaval dynasty, 11th -12th century A.D. in temples. Samples of lime mortar from Kausambi and Bhitari have been examined by Dr. B.B. Lal, Prakash and Rawat, Sanaullah and others, and published by A. Ghosh, H.C. Bhardwaj and others in *An Encyclopaedia of India Archaeology,* New Delhi 1989.

Therefore, more than a thousand years before the Sultans of Delhi, the Hindus had used the lime (*chūnam*) mortar on a large scale in their constructions. Lime mortar, both rough and fine, the former used for bonding bricks and stones, and the latter for plastering walls and floors, was used for the last 5000 years in India from the north to the south and from east to the west. Is it, therefore, not at all correct to say that the lime-mortar was introduced in India by the Sultans of Delhi? It is nothing but pure and simple falsehood.

3. Use of the so-called 'muslim' glazed ware in India: Sultanate or Pre-Sultanate? found in India, Sri Lanka, Pakistan, Iran, Iraq, and other countries of West Asia from 8th century A.D. onwards

The third objection raised by Habib is "the finding of medieval ('Muslim') glazed ware beneath all the floors levels, including the floors attributed to the temples by the Archaeological Survey of India in its Report."

The fact of the matter is that glazed ware was produced in India first during the Harappan times at Harappa and Mohenjodaro in the third millennium B.C. The glazed ware of greenish blue colour was used in India during the Kushana period, 1st-3rd century A.D. at Mathura. At Shah-ji-ki-Dheri the Buddhist structures used even glazed tiles. A Buddhist shrine near Dal Lake in Srinagar had courtyard paved with tiles of different colours. So was the façade of this structure. Hieun T'sang had seen many places in northern India where coloured tiles were used in the roof. The pre-Sultanate glazed pottery is found in

Gaur and Pandua in Bengal. The blue, turquoise blue, and polychrome glazed wares, i.e., potteries used in everyday life, including those which have in addition incised pictures of lotus petals, birds, etc. on them, were used throughout the Western Coast of India in the wake of the so called 'Arab Trade', from the 8th century A.D., i.e., at least 400 to 300 years before the coming of the Delhi Sultans. Glazed Wares, it is common knowledge, were produced in Iran during the pre-Islamic period, under the Sassanian rule. It is indeed called 'Sassanian Glazed Ware'. The Muslims when they came to Iran adopted it. In any case, the so-called Muslim Glazed Wares are found at the hinterland sites also, where they had reached through the Northern Trade Routes, the Uttarapath. In my own excavations conducted at Sanjan, an early Parsi site, dated to 9th -10th centuries, near Mumbai, I found them in profusion and in vast variety, and published them in *Puratattva* No. 32 (2002-2003), *History Today*, Volume 3 (2002) and *Journal of the Indian Ocean Archaeology*, No.1, 2004. Does the presence of these wares in later periods prove that these wares were *introduced* in India by the Sultans of Delhi? It is, therefore, clear that the presence of the so-called Medieval Glazed wares at the Ramajanmabhumi site will neither shift the dates of the temples from the 10th century to the 13th century nor will it prove the non-existence of the temples at the site during the pre-16th century period.

It must also be noted that there is nothing like 'Muslim Glazed Ware' and 'Hindu Glazed Ware"; glazing found on burnt earthen pots and pans was primarily a technique which was adopted by many people in India and West Asia from very early times as noted above. What is, however, sometimes called 'Medieval' or 'Muslim' Glazed Ware is the one which was produced in Iraq, Iran, Syria, etc. in West Asia from the 8th - 9th centuries, at sites like Basra in Iraq, and Siraf and Nishapur in Iran but taken to many parts of the world by the Arab traders. This ware is also called 'South Mesopotamian Islamic Turquoise Grey Ware', sometimes even 'Hib' Ware and 'Sassanian-Islamic Blue Glazed Pottery' by scholars like R.E. Mason and A. Rougeulle. Ian Glover has also written long articles on these 'Muslim' Glazed Wares. A.V. Sedov has written a whole book on this subject. The so-called 'Muslim Glazed Ware' has also been found at Mantai in Sri Lanka, which has been mentioned by J. Carswell and M. Prickett in *Ancient Ceylon*, No. 5, 1984. They have found it at 25 sites in India also.

Therefore, it is not at all correct to say that the so-called 'Muslim' Glazed Ware came to India with the Sultanate. It had a long history in India as in many other countries in the east, upto China and Japan, belonging to the pre-Sultanate times. Irfan Habib could not be more wrong.

4. Imagining pre-Baburi Sultanate period Qanātī-mosque at Rama Janmabhumi! Do the structural remains prove it at all?

The fourth point relates to the discovery of a 'Massive Structure' of a temple 'below the Disputed Structure', mentioned in the Report. In this context Habib observes that this wall must have belonged to a 'mosque', a pre-Mughal mosque, of the Sultanate period. Thus, in order to counter the evidence of the existence of two temple-complexes at the site, one belonging to the 10th century A.D. and the other belonging to the 12th century A.D., as proved by the ASI Report, Habib has concocted the theory of 'Two Mosques', one built after the other (first during the Delhi Sultanate period to which the 'Massive Wall', according to him, belonged, and the second in the early 16th century, 1528-29 A.D. by Babur), although, in the absence of any solid evidence in his favour, he took recourse to utter falsehood to the extent of charging the Archaeological Survey of India of even removing the evidence, destroying the evidence and manipulating the evidence, such as 'ignoring' Mihrāb' in the *Qanātī* Mosque, creating pillar-bases where there were none and calling the Islamic Tomb a Hindu Shrine. We wish all these charges were true!

The falsehood of Qanātī mosque: He observes, 'It is obvious from the presence of lime-mortar and attached walls that floor 4, the lowest floor, belongs to Sultanate period (i.e., 1206 A.D.- 1526 A.D.). *A mihrāb having been found in an attached wall* (ignored in the Report), it is certain, that it belongs to a pre-Mughal open (qanātī) mosque or īdgāh.'

In other words, there is a wall attached to the 'massive wall' of the 12th century temple which is being projected by Habib as *Qanātī mosque*. What indeed a great discovery! Just a simple 'attached wall', to the main wall, meaning a secondary wall, being interpreted as *Qanātī* mosque. And for this purpose he even goes to the extent of imagining the existence of a *mihrāb* in this wall, which simply does not exist; the charge of 'ignoring' it in the Report is absolutely baseless, biased and falsehood since in the process of actual excavations as well as in writing of this report there were at least four Muslim archaeologists but not one of them recorded it. There was neither a *Qanātī mosque* here nor *mihrāb* in any wall, 'attached' or 'independent'. It is all imaginning things which never existed at the site. Neither the ASI Report supports it nor the actual remains of structures at the site, on which in any case the 'Report' in based. It is not supported by even the Muslim traditional accounts, written or oral, contemporary or later. Who built the *Qanātī* mosque? When exactly was it built? What are its details? A *Qanātī* mosque should have several *mihrābs,* and in odd numbers, one alone, if it was at all there, will not do.

It is in fact just a fabricated story and nothing else. There is only the lower portion of a recessed nich of rectangular shape. There is no arch here (Vol. II of the Report, Plate XLIX, 49).

5. Questioning the very existence of pillar-bases: negationism of historians: How else in any case a large building can be erected?

Irfan Habib wants us to believe that there were no 'pillar-bases' at the excavated site, all the 50 'pillar-bases' were only 'plugged up' 'hollows' for making a floor. This is his fifth howler. Poor historian trying to project himself an archaeologist.

The ASI Report makes mention of 50 pillar-bases found in the excavations. Prof. B.B. Lal had found six of them in 1970s. Hence these are not new discoveries, only their number has increased since the area covered for excavations has increased. These 'bases' belong to two different periods, four to the earlier (10th century) and 46 to the later (12th century). For the earlier period Radiocarbon dates have also been quoted in the Report. In fact, there are as many as ten C-14 dates from various levels.

Why so few of the pillar-bases of the 10th century A.D. asks Habib? Those who have even the elementary knowledge of archaeological excavations, unfortunately Habib does not possess it since he has never excavated a single site in his life, will understand the fact that unless the structures and floors of the later period are removed bodily, one can not find the structures and floors of the earlier periods buried beneath them. The strategy adopted by archaeologists is simple: leave the maximum amount of the evidence of the later period, i.e., of the upper levels, and go down only in available areas to find out the clues of earlier structures and floors. This was exactly what the excavators did at Ayodhya. They left behind 46 pillar-bases intact, and can still be seen *in situ* by every one. Then in the limited area available to them they had dug below the level of 46 bases. In this limited excavated area they naturally found very few pillar-bases, only four of them; this level belonged to the 10th century. What is surprising in it? Had they removed the 46 bases and then gone down the floors associated with them, they would have certainly found many more of them.

Unexcavated area: Moreover, it should be clearly noted that the entire area of the present-day 'Rāma Lalā make-shift platform' was left out from excavations under the orders of the Hon'ble High Court because that would have meant the removal of the idols, a step not found prudent by the Court itself.

Further, the life of this 10th century temple may have been as long as 150 to 200 years, said to be 'short lived', because generally temples last for 500 years or more if not deserted or destroyed. Irfan Habib has mischieveously called it 'incomplete'. But this is besides the point.

A Funny question: It appears that Lime Mortar is haunting Irfan Habib so much that in his write-up he has raised it in various ways repeatedly at various places. He has asked a funny question whose answer is, however, inbuilt, 'They (46 pillar-bases) contain not only mud bonding but also lime mortar and *thus follow Muslim methods of construction.* Are we, then, to suppose, following the ASI's inferences, that the great temple was built under Muslim rulers, the Delhi Sultans and the Sharqi rulers of Jaunpur?'

As noted above, lime mortar was used for both the purposes in the Harappan Period (3000 B.C.), Mauryan Period (300 B.C.), Sunga Period (200 B.C.), Kushana Period (1st century A.D.), Gupta Period (5th century A.D.) and Pre-Sultanate Period (8th -12th century). It is, therefore, evident that there is absolutely no truth in the observation of Irfan Habib.

More on pillar-bases: Irfan Habib goes on to say that 'the 50 pillar bases are the *only argument* left for a temple, even if 46 of these have to be dated to the Sultanate times'. Is it so? What about the carved structural pieces depicting motifs associated with temples in India? Are the photographs of these pieces not there in the ASI Report? Also, do they not match with those temple pieces which were discovered earlier (June 1992), on display in the local U.P. State Museum at Ayodhya, December 1992 and January 1993 kept in lock-and-key at Ayodhya by the Commissioner, Faizabad? We suggest to Habib to look into the older reports and publications also before making such non-scholarly remarks.

Supression of facts: The Discovery of an Āmalaka: A sure sign of the existence of a North Indian Temple: Secondly, let us make is absolutely clear, that the '50 pillar-bases' alone were not cited in the Report as evidence for the existence of two temples at the site. The excavators have quoted the evidence of the discovery of an ***āmalaka*** at the site which is exclusively used in the *śikharas* (spires) of north Indian temples. Do we take it that the *āmalakas* were used in secular Hindu buildings also? Irfan Habib, who is crying foul, has willfully suppressed this evidence simply because it is inconvenient to him.

Supression of facts: The idol of divine couple, sure sign of a temple: Then, the discovery of a highly damaged icon of a 'Divine Couple' at Rama Janmabhumi, presumably of Umā-Maheshvara, has also been suppressed by Habib. Are we to suppose that this icon was worshipped in a mosque and not in a Hindu temple?

Supression of facts: The sacred motifs on carved stones, sure signs of a temple: Then, the discovery of ***makara*** or crocodile image, used variously as a *vāhana* of Ganga, as the symbol of water fecundity, as the mouth of *pranāla* in a temple, has also been suppressed by him. Do we take this sculptural piece in black stone as the one used by Delhi Sultans and Sharqi rulers of Jaunpur in one of their mosques? The *makara* formed the *pranāla* or water chute in a shrine with a deity on which milk and water are poured in *abhisheka* ritual; it is hollow from inside so that the liquid is taken out of the shrine.

There are many other sacred motifs found carved on stone pieces, quoted and illustrated by the excavators in their Report in favour of a temple, for example meandering creeper called ***vallarī***, lotus ***kamala*** or ***padma***, lozenges with flowers ***maṇi ratna,*** divine beings called ***yakshas***, and several others. Stylistically, all these examples of works of art are found earlier also at the site and widely published.

Supression of facts: More on 'pillar-bases,' sure signs of a temple: Irfan Habib is so much haunted by the pillar-bases that he further observes, 'These are curious 'pillar-bases', indeed, in that they have no associations with any pillar!' What is 'curious' about it, the discovery of a fragment of a black stone pillar with eight facets (published in Vol. II, Plate *LXXVii*, No. 84) has been intentionally suppressed by the worthy scholar. It may be recalled that as many as 14 similar pillars were present in the disputed structure before 6th December 1992. Two more were there at the grave of Mūsā Ashīkān, less than a km away from the Ramajanmabhumi site on its west. One more was there in a triangular park in Faizabad cantonment, of late shifted in the house of a Military Officer.

Calcrete stone and sandstone slabs on top of the 'pillar-bases'? A falsehood aglore: In the same context, he further observes, ' They generally comprise calcrete stones resting on loose or *mud bonded brickbats.* How such a 'base' could ever carry a stone or brick pillar that has fancy drawings. It would have been a shaky structure indeed, which was held up by pillars resting on heaps of brickbats at different levels'. What could be a greater contradiction. Second first.

Habib appears to have forgotten what he wrote in earlier passages. He had said that these 'bases' belonged to the Sultanate Period since it was the rulers of this dynasty who according to him, brought in the technology of lime-mortar. If so, why should these be 'mud-bonded'? Why did they discard lime mortar in this case? Where else the Sultans used mud mortar? Did they use it at Delhi where they had erected so many mosques, *mīnārs* and *makbarās?*

At another place he observed that these 'bases' were the 'filled-up hollows' in the floor. Then why should the brickbats be bonded at all even with mud? The fact is that it is all a big lie and his observations are full of contradictions.

It may be seen from several photographs published by the excavators in Vol. II of the Report (Plates *XXXVii*, No. 37; *XXXViii*, No. *XXXIX*, No. 39) that the brick pillar-bases, unless disturbed and robbed, were either fully encased from all the sides, including the top surface, by stone slabs or orthostats, or else topped by a single piece of carved stone. Therefore, let it be clearly understood that there was absolutely no question of their inherent weakness'they were quite capable of carrying weight of the black stone (*kasauṭī*) pillars of not more than six feet in height, one of which was found in the excavations and published with the details of a *kalaśa* or *pūrṇa-ghaṭa*, floral design, dancing figures, lotus flowers and *yaksha* images, etc. all Hindu sacred motifs (Vol. II, Plate LXXVi, No. 82).

Let us look at his still further observations in this context, 'Not only are they badly aligned, *if aligned at all*, these pillars are *sealed* by, they themselves *pierce*, either Floor 3 or Floor 2 of the mosque'. So the cat is out of the bag. The poor man, after all Irfan Habib, who is only a historian, is unable to distinguish the archaeological feature of 'sealed by' from the archaeological feature of 'pierceing floors' (Floor 3 or Floor 2 of the so-called mosque). Which 'mosque', the 'concocted one', of the 11th-12th century (dated by him to Sultanate Period) one or the so-called 'Baburi Mosque' of the 16th century? He has cleverly avoided this. If it was the so-called 'Baburi Mosque', then it may be noted that it had three floors, viz. IA, IB and IC. But if it was the 'imagined' one, it was floor 3. Since he talks of Floor 2 and Floor 3, it is presumed that he talks of the 'Imagined Mosque' which was in fact a temple.

Since we firmly assert that there has never been any literary or traditional account in favour of the existence of two mosques at the site of Ramajanmabhumi, and there is also no archaeological evidence of the 'imagined mosque' of the Sultanate Period either'no fragment of any Persian or Arabic inscription, no remains of Qiblah, no remains of minarates, no remains of domes, no remains of mihrāb, no remains of piers, in fact no remains of any architectural member of a mosque, let it be made absolutely clear that the Floors 2 and 3 were laid against the structures of the temples with pillars.

Our answer to his still further observation that 'The fact is that these are neither 'pillar bases' nor 'structural bases' is that this kind of negationism does not apply to archaeologically excavated remains since they still exist at the site and can be verified again and again; their photographs, published in the Report, can also been seen. Archaeology is not history, it is science, archaeological remains are material remains hence they have plastic quality, hence constantly verifiable by seeing and touching.

The trouble with most of the historian, in India, particularly those dealing with medieval history, is that hardly any one has proper training in field-archaeology.

6. An Anthropologist projected as 'experienced archaeologist': the propounder of 'hollow'theory and hollow claims

Look here what great authority Irfan Habib is quoting in favour of his wild charges against the ASI excavations and in favour of his imagined pre-Baburi Sultanate period Mosque. He starts the paragraph with 'To my friend Dr. Ashok Dutta of Kolkata, an experienced archaeologist, I owe the most satisfactory explanation'. Datta has been quoted as saying 'They (pillar-bases) are remains of brickbats put into *hollows* of ground in order to make it level.' Which 'hollows'? Who had made them? How were they formed? What was their shape? How deep were they? Why are they jutting out? Why were they arranged in rows? And 46 of them placed at almost equi-distance of around 3.5 metres. What a great coincidence! You call them non-aligned! In fact it is outright fraud played on unsuspected mass media! They are pillar-bases and they were arranged according to well-laid plans of the temples with halls or *maṇḍapas.* Use the compass and you will find them neatly arranged in cardinal directions.

The calcrete and sandstone slabs on top of the pillar-bases: Look what he writes further! 'Calcrete stones were *put at the top to press them into place,* and then the floor was laid out.' It implies the presence of stone slabs on the top of all the pillar-bases. The pillar-bases were not only generally topped by sandstone slabs but the four sides were also veneered by similar slabs or orthostats of sandstone as may be clearly seen in the photographs published in Vol. II of the Report (Plates XXXVII; XXXVIII), already mentioned. The orthostats were made of both kinds of stone, calcrete as well as sandstone. Thus, it is more than clear that the pillar-bases were very strong and could easily carry the weight of the pillars. No archaeologist in the world has ever reported 46 hollows in a floor filled with bricks bonded with clay.

Flooring and reflooring: sure sign of the existence of two temples: Habib observes: 'As time passed and the mosque, (presumably the Imagined one of the Sultanate period) had to be refloored, *brickbats were again put in to close holes and depressions* in the old floor in order to lay out a new one', presumably Floor 2 which was found directly below the lowest floor (IC) of the so-called Baburi Mosque. That is why they are all over the place and under practically all the floors, and so at different levels'.

In this context it may be noted that the Floor 3 was laid *against* the four pillar-bases of the 10th century temple. Pillar-bases, let it be clearly understood, are structures which partially jet out their floors and partly sunk in specially made pits; the pits are made first, then the bases are made and finally floors are laid against them. After nearly 150 to 200 years, in the 12th century a new temple was built here, 84 pillar-bases were erected of which 46 have been excavated, and new floor was laid *against* them. Thus, floors were laid *against* the pillar-bases each time a new temple was made. However, when a new temple was to be built, and for this purpose a new floor was laid, the entire area was levelled with brickbats, etc. filling the spaces between the two pillar-bases which were jetting out. There is nothing surprising in it. But will this normal practice make it a mosque?

The Non-existence of 'heaps' of brickbats: To quote one other uncharitable observation. 'The ASI simply ignored those *heaps* which its team considered too far out of 'alignment' for such heaps.' This is simply an uncalled for allegation against a team of 25 practicing field-archaeologists of the country by an anthropologist Ashok Dutta and a historian Irfan Habib. To say that the 50 pillar-bases could not 'sustain', 'pillars', 'they only provided level ground for mosque flooring' is the height of ignorance. 'Hollows', 'brickbats', 'all over', 'heaps of brickbats', pressed by 'calcrete stones', 'brickbats put to close holes and depressions' are the products of wild imaginations, neither the published 'plans' of different excavated levels in as many as 90 trenches, nor 'sections' running through them and published in the *Report* even remotely suggests what the observer will like us to believe. It is not only unsound archaeology, it is totally bogus archaeology.

7. A 10th century circular structure: Hindu shrine fancifully interpreted as Muslim tomb with falsehood as the only justification

And finally the tail end of the write-up of Irfan Habib.

"I end with another absurdity", presumably of the ASI Report. "Much is made out of the "Circular Shrine" (Report, pp. 70-71) with fanciful drawings (Figs. 24 and 24A). Comparisons with other circular Hindu shrines are made (Fig. 18) though not, of course, with any circular domed buildings! When a careful reader looks at the Plan of the Circular Shrine on Fig. 17, thankfully drawn to scale, its total diameter (inclusive of the thick wall) is found to be just 180 cms or less than 6 feet! Moreover, the wall does not even make quarter of a circle, so that even this smallest of 'Circular shrines' is just a piece of the ASI's own imagination'.

Is this academics? The facts are as follows.

There is, on the southern side of the site, a circular structure of burnt bricks (sizes: 28x21x5.5cm. and 22x18x5.5cm.) laid in several courses, as many as thirteen of them found *in situ*. From inside it is square. The outer diameter is less than 6 ft. The inside square space is around 4.4 ft. in length and breadth. The entrance to this structure is from the east. For this purpose a rectangular projection was made. The door-sill was laid with a calcrete stone slab. On the north side there is water chute or *pranāla* for the removal of water from inside the shrine.

The excavators feel that it was a small shrine. Abhisheka of the deity was done with water and milk because of the water-chute (*pranāla*) on the north, which can clearly be seen in Plate LX, No. 60 of Vol. II of the Report. With the Muslim Agenda in hand, Irfan Habib declares this shrine as 'tomb'. The question is whose tomb it was? Then, could such a small structure of around 4.3 ft. from inside contain the dead body of a man laid in extended position? Where is the dead-body? And on top of all this, is there any example in northern India, of the Sultanate and the Mughal periods, i.e., the entire Muslim period, in which a tomb is built of burnt bricks and whose roundedness starts from the ground level itself? How will a dome then be raised over this structure? Where are the piers? Let me categorically state that it could never be a tomb. The historian Irfan Habib seems to know nothing of the Tomb architecture.

8. Muslim tomb or Buddhist stupa? ridiculous claims

Of late, some of our historian friends have come out with a new theory, that if the circular structure was not a tomb, it may have been a Buddhist stupa. However, it appears that they do not know that a stupa is a solid structure and it has absolutely no chamber in the centre, much less with an entrance from any direction to reach the core area on regular basis. India has no example of this kind.

Apparently, we suspect that these scholars have some axe to grind.

9. The communal compulsion of communist Irfan Habib: the 'two mosques' theory and a bundle of lies: the inside story

The question is as to why Irfan Habib is trying his level best to identify the circular Hindu shrine as a Muslim 'tomb'? It is very simple.

Habib wants to prove that the Baburi Mosque was built on plain grassy ground where at best cattle used to graze, and not on the debris of a temple. This is exactly the Muslim stand and pleading in the present-day litigation. Now how can this be proved archaeologically? Therefore, first he made a theory, the theory that the 'Massive Wall' along with its 'attached' wall represents not a temple but a mosque. Then he dated it to the Sultanate Period. Since there are absolutely no remains of a regular mosque of this period at the site, no dome, no *kiblah*, etc. he had no other option but to call it a *Qanātī* mosque in which one needs only a wall with, of course, *mihrabs*, not one but three or five or seven or even more of them. So, this is the Compulsion of Irfan Habib. He is falsifying all kinds of histories, including the history of

Muslim Architecture in India, 'Muslim' Glazed Ware in India, Lime Mortar and Plaster used in Indian Art and Architecture, presence of Animal Bones in Temple debris and the presence of 50 Pillar-Bases at Ramajanmabhumi.

This is the most dirty trick that a motivated historian plays for short-term publicity. In anycase, this is the inside story of imaginning two mosques at Ramjanmabhumi, one belonging to the Sultanate Period (Habib has not dated this mosque precisely anywhere in his write-up, he only talks of the Sultanate Period, which covers a period of at least 300 years (1206-1526 A.D.) on his own admission but imposed on a 12th century 'massive structure' of a temple, and the other of the Mughal Period of 16th century. However, for the last 400 years the world knew only of the 16th century so-called Baburi Mosque at Ramajanmabhumi, but now Habib has taken out of his hat a Sultanate Period mosque also which, however, never existed.

Irfan Habib's present write-up has thus completely discredited his own scholarship which, of course, was never there in the field of archaeology.

The right approach

Archaeology is a multi-disciplinary science. Its sources are in the explored and excavated remains materials which are verifiable again and again by one and all. It employs several scientific methods of dating, including the well known Radiocarbon method. The data-recording method is Three Dimensional, hence accurate. It also employs Art Historical Method to date sculptures and structures. It is, therefore, surprising as to why Marxist and Communal historians are making a big hue and cry over the ASI Report (2002-2003) on Ayodhya. Afterall the site was subjected to excavations even previously. It was dug by Prof. A.K. Narain in 1970; by Prof. B.B. Lal from 1975 through 1980, by PWD in June 1992, by S.P. Gupta and K.M. Srivastava in July-August 1992. These were physically examined by 40 scholars from all over the country who assembled at Ayodhya in October 1992 to attend a three-days conference on the history and archaeology of Ayodhya under the banner of Indian History & Culture Society. Even on 6th December 1992 a lot of material of antiquarian value came to light. In January 1993 also an *āmalaka* was found buried in a pit by the labour engaged in erecting a barricade in the presence of high-ranking officers of the Civil and Police Administration.

Much of these material items unearthed at Ramajanmabhumi have been published variously in several volumes of *Indian Archaeology-A Review*, a Govt. of India (ASI) annual publication besides the highly-illustrated book in Hindi, entitled *Ayodhyā kā Itihāsa aivam Purātattva* by T.P. Verma and S.P. Gupta.

The archaeological, art, architectural and epigraphical remains are housed in the Department of History, Culture and Archaeology, Banaras Hindu University, Archaeological Survey of India, Purana Qila, New Delhi, Ramayana Research Institute and Museum, Ayodhya, and the New Police Building, Ayodhya (under the charge of the Commissioner, Faizabad).

The main findings in them include:

1. A 20 line Sanskrit inscription written in 11th - 12th century script called 'Nāgarī.'
2. Two fragmentary inscriptions on a part of a stone pillar in the same language and script.
3. A fragmentary inscription in Arabic script of 16th century.
4. Black stone pillars decorated with Hindu motifs such as lotus, dancing figures, peacock, sacred water-pitchers, *yakshas,* etc.
5. Architectural pieces of a temple decorated with-Hindu motifs, such as the *āmalaka, chhādya,* door-jamb, capitals, etc.
6. Two diamond shaped motifs *mani-ratna* found carved on architectural pieces.

In them the 20 line inscription is most important because of the following reasons:

a) It is a contemporary written record hence most reliable and clinching evidence notwithstanding the accusing fingers of some motivated scholars.

b) It can be precisely dated because it was engraved during the reign of Emperor Govinda Chandra of the Gahadvala Dynasty whose period of rule is well known in history: 1114 A.D.-1154 A.D.
c) It mentions the erection of a temple dedicated of Lord Vishṇu-Hari.
d) The identification of the Lord Viṣṇu-Hari is also given in the same text 'He was the one who had humbled the pride of Rājā Bali and killed Dashānana', i.e., Rāvaṇa. Clear enough, he could be none else than Rāma, an incarnation of Lord Vishṇu.

7. The second most important find is *āmalaka* since it is found exclusively on the top of the *shikharas* on the North Indian temples.
8. The third important excavated item was the discovery of as many as six 'pillar-bases' in the southern trenches on Ramajanmabhumi dug by B.B. Lal in 1975-'80.
9. The fourth significant find includes several sacred motifs carved on stone pieces used in temples such as the *yaksha, kalaśa* or *Pūrṇa-ghaṭa,* and *padma.*

The ASI Report makes mention of the following finds:

1. A fragmentary inscription in Nāgarī script of 12th century.
2. Two fragmentary inscriptions in Arabic script of the 16th century.
3. An *āmalaka.*
4. A lotus bearing carved stone.
5. A meandering creeper or *vallarī* carved on stone.
6. Two diamond shaped *motifs* with carved flowers inside.

If we, therefore, look at the findings mentioned in the ASI Report 2002-2003 it will become quite clear that except for a few new discoveries such as the Circular Shiva Temple and a few sacred motifs on stone pieces such as the *makara,* nothing is new; all others were discovered earlier also.

CONCLUSION

If so, then what is the value of this ASI Report?

The ASI Report of 2003 has the supreme value in corroborating the archaeological and art-historical findings of the earlier regular excavations and casual diggings mentioned above. For example, the fragmentary Nāgarī inscription of the Report corroborates the inscriptions found earlier. The *āmalakas* found earlier are exactly of the same type as has been found in the present excavations. The lotus symbol is also found depicted in identical style. The *vallarī* or meandering creeper is also exactly the same as was found earlier.

Thus, as noted above, the supreme value of the ASI Report 2002-2003 lies not so much in digging out new things as in corroborating the old findings made by several scholars in the past. It has, therefore, stamped the final seal of approval of the so far held views that at Ramajanmabhumi there did exist a temple of the 12th century A.D. which was destroyed in order to build the disputed structure of the so-called 'Baburi Mosque' directly on the ruins of the temple.

Miḥrāb or Niche (*Ālaya*) Discovered in Recent Ayodhya Excavations?

R. Nath*

The lowest part of a recessed niche has been discovered in the recent excavations at Ayodhya *(The Archaeological Survey of India Report* 2002-2003, submitted to the High Court Allahabad, Plate-49: 'A Niche in the north-south oriented brick wall' TR-ZE2). It is built of brick masonry which was plastered over. Its plan is rectangular with a single recess (offset) making a *karṇikā* (corner) in it. Its floor is also of brick and it is three courses (of brick masonry) higher than the floor-level of the room on which it opens, and of which it is a part.

This has been identified by Irfan Habib as a *miḥrāb* which 'belongs to a pre-Mughal open (*qanātī*) mosque or *'īdgāh'*. This claim warrants a careful scrutiny.

It must be noted, pre-eminently, that it is a single niche, given in the N-S wall, with no arches or similar niches on its sides. One wonders if he means to say that this *qanātī* mosque or *īdgāh* had only a single arch. A *qanātī* (so called because it has a *'qanātī'* or series of arches) mosque or *īdgāh* invariably has a series of arches in odd number, e.g. 3,5,7,9 or 11. In India, such an open 'curtain' mosque which does not have a *'līwān'* (prayer-hall) or any other paraphernalia attached to it, and is just a wall, has 5 or 7 or 11 arches, as a rule, and a single arch cannot make-up a *'qanātī'* mosque. Technically, it is an arcade and such arcade-walls were built in *īdgāhs* and graveyards for facilitating *fatiha* prayer, during the whole medieval period (1192-1803 A.D.). A single arch, even if it was there, cannot be branded a *'qanātī'* mosque or *īdgāh*, and his claim shows that he is not, at all, conversant with the subject.

Secondly, that a *qiblah miḥrāb* (an arch in the centre of the western wall of a tomb or mosque, denoting the direction of the *ka'bah'*) is an arch, roofed by a half-cup shaped vault, both of which have tremendous lateral thrust. Hence, stone nook-shafts are invariably used on the corners of such a *miḥrāb*, as are there in the mosques of Jaunpur and Delhi (of the Sultanate period, 1192-1526 A.D.), for example, without any exception. But lithic nook-shafts are not there on the corners of this niche. It is architecturally inconceivable to build an arch, roofed by a vault, in a brick masonry without stone nook-shafts, and if stone nook-shafts are not there to take the load, and counter the lateral thrust of the arch and vault, there cannot be a *miḥrāb*. Structurally, therefore, there was no arch or vault, and it was just a single, rectangular

*Former Professor & Head of History Dept., Rajasthan University, Jaipur

niche- which is what the *Archaeological Survey of India Report* says.

It has also to be noticed, thirdly, that the floor-level of this niche is three courses higher than the floor-level of the room on which it opens. This is possible only when it was made as a niche or *'ālaya'* for placing an image, or for a similar other purpose. The *miḥrāb* and the *līwān* (sanctuary or prayer-hall of a mosque) are always, and without any exception, built on the same floor-level, and there is not a single example where a *miḥrāb* is built on a higher level as a niche for keeping things. Hence this cannot be identified as a *miḥrāb*, in any case.

Irfan Habib is an eminent scholar of international repute of Economic History of Mughal India and he has specialized in this discipline. His claim, as discussed above, proves that he has no grounding in, and no acquaintance with, the medieval architecture of India, in which discipline his amateurish opinion is hardly tenable.

Lime Mortar, Plaster and Surkhī in Ancient India

H.C. Bhardwaj*

Amongst the building materials, mortars and plasters are important ingredients. Mortar may be defined as a material used for bedding and joining or cementing the building materials, such as bricks and stones. Plaster is the material used for coating walls, ceiling, floors, etc. Sometimes the same material may be used as mortar as well as plaster but mortar is generally coarser in texture than plaster. In ancient times mortars were very thick and rich lime but since it was mixed with sand containing larger or smaller sizes of grains of silica, the mortar was coarse or fine, respectively. Sometimes pozzolanic material was mixed in lime; this material was *Surkhī*, etymologically 'red', because it was crushed, powdered, and kiln-fired bricks. In addition, organic materials such as straw, twigs, and leaves, etc. are mixed, so as to modify the pore-structure of the mortar which increased its durability.

Lime is produced by burning *kankar*, calcium and magnesium rocks such as chalk, limestone, dolomite, marl, etc. It is also produced by grinding or burning oyster shell, conch, etc. Though gypsum and lime plaster/mortar have been used during antiquity, the evidence of the earliest use of lime and gypsum comes from the sites of the Indus Civilization.

Neolithic Period: 3500 B.C.

At Gufkral, Dist. Anantnag, Kashmir[1], we get the evidence of a 70 cm. wall made of compact clay mixed with lime in Period IB datable to Neolithic period of the early fourth millennium B.C.

Harappan Period: 3000-2000 B.C.

At Kalibangan, Distt. Hanumangarh, Rajasthan[2], use of lime plaster is noticed in the drains within the houses belonging to Period I of Early Harappan phase datable to 3000 B.C.-2700 B.C.

At Harappa on the Ravi[3], belonging to late 3rd millennium B.C. gypsum and lime mortars were used in certain buildings. It consists of variable mixture of sand (20% to 40%), gypsum (45% to 75%) and lime (2% to 25%). Lime mortar, with sizeable percentage of magnesium, is also used in the Indus cities. It contains calcium carbonate (26% to 57%), magnesium carbonate (4% to 11%) and sand clay (34% to 61%). The high percentage of sand and clay in lime plaster,

*Former Professor, Dept. of AIHC&A, B.H.U., Varanasi

however, suggests that it was prepared by burning *kankar* (calcarious nodules). The use of lime mortar was, by and large, restricted to drains and floors of bathrooms, etc. where water was expected to flow or retained.

From the analysis of various samples of mortars and plasters from Mohenjodaro[4], in Sindh, another 3rd millennium B.C. Harappan site, it may be concluded that gypsum mortar/plaster was quite common. Lime plaster was generally mixed with gypsum, but lime plaster free from gypsum has also been reported both from Harappa and Mohenjodaro. The same was true of Kalibangan. Flinders Petrie (1909) informs us that during the same period the Egyptians also used lime mortar.

Chalcolithic Period: 2000 B.C.

The excavations at Navadatoli[5], a Chalcolithic site of Malwa, by H.D. Sankalia show that 'The *chulah* as well as the floors were thinly plastered with lime and there was clay border'. It is dated to 1505 B.C.

Lumps of finely made lime in the shape of balls have been found mostly from late Jorwe levels at sites like Inamgaon (datable to second-first millennium B.C.). Sometimes these have been carefully stored in pots. In one house of late Jorwe phase a large number of lime balls were found. This indicates that some people were engaged in the actual manufacture of lime. Significantly, a heap of shell was noticed near the house, but no kiln.

Early Iron Age: 1000 B.C.-600 B.C.

In addition to the above, mention may be made of use of clay, lime, gravel and hydraulic lime from post-Chalcolithic levels at Navasa[6]. Obviously, lime mortar/plaster was in use at Nevasa between 1000 B.C. and 600 B.C. period. During this period iron had already appeared in the metal repertoire of India.

Early Historical Period: 600 B.C.-300 A.D.

In the excavation report of Kumrahar, near Patna, Bihar[7], A.S. Altekar and V. Mishra report that 'in the ashy layer 7 of the Tomb Trench unearthed to ascertain the cause of the destruction of Mauryan pillared hall, plaster of lime and brickbats have been found. It showed that either the wooden roof or wooden floor might have been plastered with brick and lime'. This layer dates to around 2nd century B.C.

Lime mortar was used at Kausambi, near Allahabad, U.P.,[8] in the Early Historical period. It is dated from 600 B.C. to A.D. 100. The results of the chemical analysis show that the content of sand in the mortar was slightly higher than that in plaster. The average ratio of sand:lime Ca(OH)2 is about 1:1, whereas in the case of mortars the average is 2:1. For mortar, probably two parts of sand was mixed with one part of slaked lime.

At Taxila, near Islamabad, in Pakistan,[9] lime was used extensively in the buildings of the Parthian levels, 2nd century-1st century B.C. At Sirkap, in Taxila, lime was used for finishing both internal and external surfaces. Floors at Julian, Taxila, were covered with bajari-lime concrete. During the early centuries of the Christian era lime was used in several Buddhist monuments of the North-West.

At Besnagar, Dist. Vidisha, Madhya Pradesh[10] we get the evidence of use of lime in the mortar of the brick wall temple belonging to 2nd century B.C.The analysis of this mortar gave the following:

Soluble silica (8.20 %), Siliceous matter (51.60 %), Total lime (CaO- 14.11 %), Magnesia (MgO- 2.74 %), Carbonic acid (5.64 %), Oxides of Iron & Alumina (20.00) and Potassium & Sodium Chlorides (0.30 %). According to John Marshall, 'this analysis gives the idea of a well made mortar, prepared with a full recognition of the purpose served by sand and clayey matter in making the material, as well as the lime.' This mortar was used with large quantities of lime to bind bricks as has been mentioned by Percy Brown who quoted the original excavator Sir Alexander Cunningham.

While summing up his excavation at Nongarh,

Dist. Monghyr, Bihar[11], A. Cunningham wrote in his report that 'the use of mortar, lime and *soorkey* was known along with lime plastering at that early period (1st century B.C.-A.D. 1st century).'

The excavations at Mathura[12], by M.C. Joshi, has yielded the evidence of the use of lime in the plaster used for making floor on the brick pavement.

While exploring the site of Nagarjunikonda,(3rd century A.D.) Dist. Guntur, Andhra Pradesh,[13] John Marshall found a old stone mortar-wheel used for grinding shell lime for making plaster and whitewash.

Pre-Gupta, Gupta and Post-Gupta: 100-400 A.D.-700 A.D.

At Arikamedu in Pondichery,[14] lime mortar is reported from early historical period of 1st century A.D. Use of lime is also attested from Hulas Khera, District Lucknow, U.P.,[15] from Kushan-Gupta levels and from Banagarh (District Dinajpur, West Bengal[16]) where use of lime and *surkhī* is known in the Gupta (5th century) and Pala (8th century) levels.

At Purana Qila in Delhi,[17] lime plastered gutter connected with house drains is reported from levels datable to 8th -9th century A.D.

From Sarnath, District Varanasi, U.P.[18] we get the evidence of use of lime in the plaster of jambs and architraves of the chapel entrances belonging to 4th-5th century A.D.

Chemical analysis of lime plaster from Bhitari, District Gazipur, U.P.[19], belonging to the Gupta period, shows that low grade lime plaster was used in the brick temple of the Gupta period. It has sand and lime ratio of 6:1. The red colour of the plaster/mortar is due to the use of ferruginous *kankar* for the preparation of lime.

The excavations at Aphsad, District Nawadah, Bihar[20] revealed the use of lime and *surkhī* in the flooring of the paths of the Vishnu temple of later Gupta period (7th century A.D.)

From the analysis of lime mortar and lime plaster used in the famous temple-site of the 7th -8th century, Karwan, District Vadodara, Gujrat [21] it is clear that two types of plasters were used. Samples 1 to 4 represent the upper coat of the plaster and 5 to 8 represent lower rough plaster. The former has higher content of lime as compared to the latter. Fine layer was laid on the top and burnished to make it smooth and elegant. The site was excavated from 1973 to 1975 by W.H. Siddiqi and C. Margabandhu.

Early Medieval: 800 A.D.-1200 A.D.

Lime plaster from excavations at Nalanda[21] in Bihar (7th -10th century A.D.) shows three parts of lime (calcium carbonate) and two parts of sand. Some of the monasteries are thickly plastered. Jars with dried up mortar and a cell exclusively used as a cistern in Monastery No. 11 are indicative of the preparation of lime concrete locally.

At Taradih, District Gaya, Bihar [22] Period V revealed 8th-12th century A.D. Pala structures the floors of which showed use of lime and *surkhī* mortar.

Lime plaster from Lingaraj temple[23] at Bhubneswar in Orissa (10th century A.D.) when analyzed showed that lime-silica (sand) ratio was 3:1.

Chola (10th-11th century) structure used lime mortar and plasters. They show two types of mixtures, rough and fine, it has a ratio of 1:1 of lime:sand in rough plaster or mortar, and 9:1 in case of fine plaster. Nāyaka structures in Tamilnadu, on the other hand, rough plaster has 1:3 ratio of lime and sand, while fine plaster has 4:1 ratio. These are dated to the 16th century A.D.[24]

Medieval: 1200 A.D.-1700 A.D.

It may thus be noted that lime mortar as well as lime plaster were used in India continuously for the last 5000 years. When the Muslim rule in Delhi was established in the 13th century, they found the Indian masons and brick-builders using lime-based mortar and plaster on popular level. They used *kankar*, found at many drylands near rivers as the raw material to produce lime by burning it for a week or so in specially built kilns.

RESULTS OF SOME ANALYSES OF LIME MORTARS

Mohenjodaro (gypsum mortar from wall): $CaSO_4.2H_2O$, 63.25. $CaCO_3$, 1.64. Sand+clay, 31.52. Gypsum: sand, 2:1.

Mohenjodaro (lime mortar from drain): $CaSO_4.2H_2O$, tr. $CaCO_3$, 39.96. Sand+clay, 47-48. $MgCO_3$, 8.83. Lime: clay, 1:1.

Harappa (lime mortar): $CaSO_4$. 2H2O, tr. $CaCO_3$, 35.02. Sand+clay, 51.39. $MgCO_3$, 10.62, Lime:sand, 2:3.

Kausambi (plaster): $CaCO_3$, 49.17. Sand+clay, 38.09. $MgCO_3$, 2.72. Al_2O_3+Fe_2O_3, 9.67. Lime:sand, 2:3

Kausambi (mortar): $CaCO_3$, 49.97. Sand+clay, 38.09. $MgCO_3$, 2.72. Al_2O_3+Fe_2O_3, 9.67. Lime:sand, 2:3

Ajanta (rough plaster): $CaCO_3$, 1.78. Sand+clay, 60.00. $MgCO_3$, 2.00. Al_2O_3+Fe_2O_3, 27.00 Mud plaster.

Bhitari (plaster): $CaCO_3$, 13.80. Sand+clay, 73.50. $MgCO_3$, 5.42. Al_2O_3+Fe_2O_3, 8.64. Lime:sand, 1:5.

Chola (rough plaster): $CaCO_3$, 49.76. Sand+clay, 49.97. $MgCO_3$, 1.07. Al_2O_3+Fe_2O_3, 1.89. Lime:sand, 1:1.

Chola (finished plaster): $CaCO_3$, 90.72. Sand+clay, 7.02. $MgCO_3$, .077. Al_2O_3+Fe_2O_3, 1.06. Lime:sand, 12:1.

Karvan (fine plaster): $CaCO_3$, (i) 94.12. Sand+clay, 5.88; (ii) 94.28. Sand+clay, 5.27; (iii) 94.46, Sand+clay, 5.54; (iv) 94.26, Sand+clay, 5.74. (roug plaster): $CaCO_3$, (i) 25.27. Sand+clay, 74.73; (ii) 26.51. Sand+clay, 73.50; (iii) 25.55, Sand+clay, 74.47; (iv) 25.95. Sand+clay, 74.04.

References

1. Chakrabarti, D.K. *India: An Archaeological History,* 2001, p.213
2. Ghosh, A. *An Encylcopaedia of Indian Archaeology,* p.294
3. Vats, M.S. *Excavations at Harappa,* New Delhi, 1940, p.469
4. Marshall, J. *Mohenjodaro and the Indus Civilization,* London, 1931, Vol.II, p.689
5. Sankalia, H.D. *etal. Excavations at Navadatoli,* pp. 46 ff
6. Sankalia, H.D. *etal. From History to Prehistory at Nevasa (1954-56),* Poona, 1960
7. Altekar, A.S. & Misra, V. *Report on Kumrahar Excavations, (Patna) 1951-55,* (Patna, 1959), p.28
8. Sharma, G.R. *Excavations at Kauṣambi 1949-50,* Memoirs of Archaeological Survery of India, No.74
9. Marshall, J. *Taxila.* Also *Pakistan Archaeology,* No. 6, 1969, p.20. "The masonry of these walls (Pd.II, 3rd century B.C.) was characterized by rough rubble set in lime
10. Marshall, J. Excavations at Besnagar, District Monghar, *AR, ASI, 1913-14,* p.206. "The bricks were grooved to hold lime mortar"
11. Cunningham, A. Excavations at Nongarh, District Monghar, *AR, ASI, 1972-73,* Vol. VIII, pp.119-120
12. Joshi, M.C. 'Excavations at Mathura', *IAR,* 1976-77, p.55. "Significant structures were a lime plastered. Some had ....lime plastered floors..."
13. Marshall, J. 'Excavations at Nagarjunikonda, District Guntur', *AR, ASI, 1928-29,* p.103
14. Wheeler, *etal.* 'Excavations at Arikamedu', *Ancient India,* No. 2, pp.17-124
15. Singh, S.B. 'Excavations at Hulaskhera', Lucknow, *IAR,* 1965-66, p.53
16. Goswami, K.G. *Excavations at Bangarh: 1938-41,* Calcutta
17. Lal, B.B. *etal.* 'Excavations at Purana Qila', *IAR, 1972-73,* p.8
18. Marshall, J. 'Excavations at Sarnath', *AR, ASI, 1904-05,* pp.65, 68

19. Bharadwaj, H.C. *An Encylcopaedia of Indian Archaeology, (Ed-A-Ghosh)* Vol. I, p.294
20. Prasad, P.C. *'Excavations at Aphsad', IAR, 1979-80,* p.14. "The path were made of lime and *surkhi*"
21. Karanth, *etal.*, 'Petrography of Ancient Indian Lime Plaster', *Jorunal of Archaeological Science,* 1986, No. 13, pp.543-551
22. Prasad, A. *'Excavations at Taradih', District Gaya, IAR, 1981-82,* p.10. "The floor, made of broken bricks and brickbats showed the use of lime and *surkhi* mortar. Tiles were used for roofing"
23. Bhardwaj, H.C. *op.cit.*
24. Bhardwaj, H.C. *op.cit.*

Select Bibliography

1. Lal, Dr. B.B. in *Ajanta Murals* (Ed. A. Ghosh) New Delhi, 1967, p.59
2. Prakash, S. *etal.* in *Chemical Studies of Some Indian Archaeological Antiquities,* Bombay, 1965
3. Parmasivan, S. *Technical Studies in the Field of Fine Arts,* No. 5, pp.228-31
4. Sana Ullah, M. *AR ASI, 1926-27,* pp.208

Notes, News and New Source-Material

Circular Temple of Ayodhya Type Discovered at Kashipur

A brick temple, circular in plan of the 8th-9th century A.D. has been recently excavated by the author at Govisana (Kashipur, Uttaranchal). It has a gargoyle in the north and it has also a rectangular projection on the east (*IAR*, 2002-03, in the press). A *Purvābhimuka* (facing east), partly damaged, circular structure of burnt bricks has been also recently excavated by Archaeological Survey of India between the trenches E8 and F8 at Aydhoya (vide the *Archaeological Survey of India Report 202-2003).*

The bricks used here are of two sizes:28x21x5.5 cm and 22x18x5 cm. The bonding material was mud mortar. On its eastern side, there is a rectangular opening, 1.32m, in length and 32.5 cm in width, which was the entrance of the structure. A calcrete block, measuring 70x27x17 cm, has also been found here, fixed, obviously, as the door-sill.

An extremely important feature of this structure is the provision of a gargoyle *(praṇāla)* made in the northern wall. *The Archaeological Survey of India Report* records that it is 0.04 m wide and 0.53 m long, projecting 35 cm froom the northern wall of the structure. It is 'V' shaped so that water may drop a little away from the wall.

The elevation, as shown in the drawing suggests that this structure was built on a raised platform, *viz. adhiṣṭhāna*. The gargoyle, or the drain, was provided on the northern side. The structure may be dated to 9th-10th century A.D. (The Archaeological Survey of India carried out C-14 determination from this level and the calibrated date ranges between 900 A.D. and 1030 A.D.)

This was an independent miniature shrine. The architectural peculiarities suggest that, in all probability, it was Śiva temple where a Śivaliṅgam was in worship, for example, the gargoyle has been provided to drain out the milk and water offered in the *abhisheka* ceremony. Noticable is the fact that gargoyle is given on the northern side as is prescribed in the *vāstu* te

It is amazing that, in spite of all these architectural features, available *in situ*, of the Sultanate period, Irfan Habib is calling it a Muslim tomb.

Secondly, it is too small a structure for a tomb, from inside it is only 4.4. ft. square. Neither could it accommodate a grave in its interior, nor a *quiblah-*

miḥrāb on its western wall; *qiblah* was an integral and essential part of tomb-structure during the Sultanate paeriod (1192-1526 A.D.) as is illustrated by numerous examples all over northern India.

Thirdly, there is no trace of an arch required for constructing dome over the tomb. There are no nook-shafts to bear and no structural trace to suggest any lateral thrust of the *miḥrāb*. It may be noted that the sub-structure of the *miḥrāb* is built massively on the edges and the four corners, to counter the lateral thrust. One wonders, if it was a tomb without any arch or dome, and without even a grave?

Thus, on the other hand, the dimension of this structure is too small for a tomb and on the other, the gargoyle was never used in tombs while it was an integral feature of the sanctum of *Śiva* temples to drain out the water poured on the śivalings. The gargoyle is there and to deny its existence is to cast aspersions not only on 25 excavators, both Hindus' and Muslims, of the Archaeological Survey of India, 2 judges, and 500 police-men but also on a dozen nominees of the concerned parties, who were constantly present during the excavations.

D.V.Sharma

Excavation Branch II
Archaeological Survey Of India
New Delhi

Indian Folk Culture as Gleaned from Ivory Art

India is a land of rich cultural heritage. It is a receptacle of composite cultures with different religions and languages. And it also reflects 'Unity in Diversity'. Most of the people live in villages, as agriculture constitutes the main source of food and economy. The rural people form eighty percent of the country's population. The traditional tales, songs, dances, fine arts, handicrafts, structures and cultures besides beliefs and social institutions of every community or race form part and parcel of the Indian culture. Among the fine arts, the ivory art played an important role in the arts and crafts of the folk culture through the ages. Few select ivory art specimens collected from different places are described here to depict the various aspects of Indian folk art culture through religion or thematic beliefs, dress pattern and ornamentation, transportation and occupation.

The Indian villagers usually follow a religion and also pray *'gramadevatas'* (village goddesses). Mother Goddess is the Goddess of Fertility generally worshiped by the village people, especially in South India. The goddess looks after the health of the children and saves them from contagious diseases like 'smallpox' (*ammavaru*) etc. A sculpture depicting the 'Mother Goddess with Children and Two Attendants (or mothers), is a fine example of Nayaka style of ivory art. The children are depicted lifting hands and bodice of the goddess in order to suck milk from her breasts. She is a form of village goddess set up as *'gramadevata'*, she is supposed to protect the children from various types of health hazards (*balarishtas*) suffered in child-hood like measles and smallpox. The rustic appearance in the disposition of the goddess and devotees, probably female figures suggest a royal air in their looks. The colossal form of the figure in the centre distinguishing it from the figures indicates that the main image is of a goddess and thus a venerable figure. The profuse ornamentation also supports the above view. This ivory sculpture (M. No. XLVI/287) is datable to 17th century A.D. and it measures 15.4 cm. in height. (Photograph No.1).

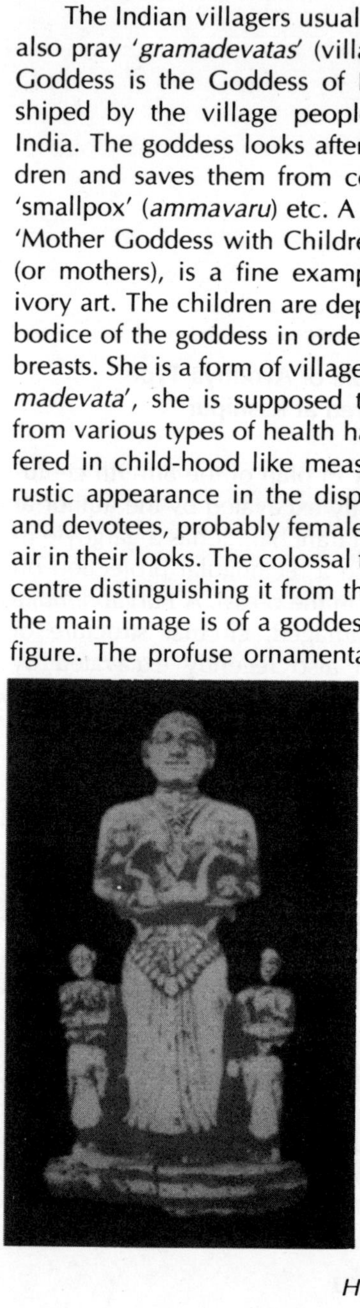

Photograph no. 1: Goddess of Fertility with child and two attendants, 17th century A.D., Tamil Nadu, Nayaka

A plain ornament without any decoration known as *'baliya,* in local parlance of *'lambada'* community is just like a ring with or without little tapering end.It is called *'balia'* irrespective of whether it is small or big. If the same is in big size it looks like a bangle and serves as bangle. It is worn on hand anywhere between arm and wrist. But when it is in small shape, it is meant conventionally for bride's dowry purpose. The custom demanded *balia* and cash in coins are to be tied in the border end of a corner of her *dupatta.* It is also informed that the usual dowry (*katnam*) given to the bridegroom is different from the said *katnam.* Since the bangle is considered as an auspicious ornament indicating her marital status, ivory banglels, which are costlier were given to the bride along with some cash. A community called *'maniars'* in Sourashtra handled the ivory whose main occupation is to make bangles. Ladies wear these bangles at their marriage and these become a part of the dowry. This custom is now given up by these tribal people because of ban on the trade of ivory. Smt. Korra Gamuri (60 years) of Loyapally village, Manchala Mandal, R.R. District possesses a *balia* in small size i.e., 2.8 cm. which was presented to her by her father in marriage along with some money about 45 years ago.

A sculpture, which represents *'bullock-cart'* with two men inside the howdah and a driver, is depicted as a common means of transport to the villagers. The two plumpy bullocks, which pull the cart look so strong and handsome that they pull the cart easily without any strain. The cart has four wheels, two on either side. The howdah in two compartments is fashioned with vaulted high ceiling structure with flower and vertical linear designs in relief. The dress of the driver denotes the characteristic costume of West Bengal. This art specimen (M.No. P5600) measures 12.5 x 8.5 cm. and is datable to 19th century A.D. It is housed in the State Museum, A.P. Hyderabad. (Photograph No.2)

Photograph no. 2: 19th century Bullockcart.

In addition to the bullocks, the man also has domesticated horses, elephants, camels etc. Such animals have been serving or helping the man to earn money by carrying howdahs, goods, pulling carts or becoming vehicles in the war etc. The Salar Jung Museum has in its collection a few examples of such means of road transport like 'A Loaded Camel' (M.No. XLVI/556) datable to 19th century A.D. The camel is carved with full load of goods on its back, which consists of a ladder, boxes, chairs, buckets and other household goods. All the household articles are tied by means of a rope so that they would not fall-down. A man probably the owner holding a stick in his left hand, stands before the animal holding its reins. He wears a heavy headgear of Delhi (or Western part of India probably Rajasthan) style with cloth twisted in several circles. A dog also accompanies the owner. The anatomical feature of all the figures in the sculpture (Photograph No.3), measuring to a height of 16.8 cm., is dexterously chiseled to provide a

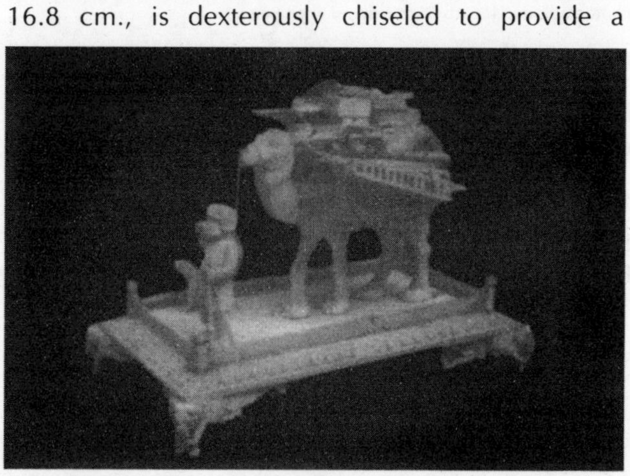

Photograph no. 3: Loaded Camel, 19th century

realistic view. An elephant also carries such household items.

'Cow and the Cowherd' (M.No. IV.4) is another specimen of a villager's representation with milk giving cow. The cowherd (*Govulakaparl*) is clad in dhoti. He wears a sash turban on his head. He may be owner of the animal. The cow with milky udder is taller than the cowherd. Before the cow, there is a basket on the ground probably full of food (*dana*). It seems the animal is tied with a rope and fastened to a hook. The sculpture is said to have come from West Bengal. This beautiful sculpture which measures 7x9cm., is on display in the Birla Museum, Hyderabad. (Photograph No.4).

Photograph no. 4: Early 20th century West Bengal

Thus, these ivory objects help us to understand the religious beliefs, modes of transportation, head-dresses etc. of the 17th-19th century Deccan.

Balagouni Krishna Goud

Salar Jung Museum,
Hyderabad

NEWS

New Findings at Hathab, Gujarat

Recently, a large Indo-Roman site has been excavated. It is called 'Hathab' located on the Arabian coast, in the district Bhavnagar, southern Gujarat. The site has been excavated by Ms. Shubhra Pramanik of the Archaeological Survey of India.

Historical Background of Hathab:

Hathab is the ancient city of Astakapra, located on the eastern coast of the Gulf of Khambat, 24 kms south of Bhavnagar. *Periplus of Erythrean Sea,* a travelogue of the 1st century A.D. by an Alexandrian Greek, is a veritable mine of information of ports and commodities of trade during that period. Hathab has also been identified with Hastakavapra, a name that occurs in a copper plate grant of Dhruvasena I of Vallabhi and also on a 'Gold Signet Ring' datable to the 4th and 5th centuries A.D. The excavations have unearthed a city dating to the early historical period. Evidence points to the existence of town planning and a mud-fort that is substantiated further by similar references in literary texts. The value of this find is greatly enhanced by the recovery of a rich collection of iron and copper implements, tools, weapons, domestic utensils, ornaments, toilet articles, coins, gold and shell jewellery, toys and other small objects, besides ancient mines and shell manufacturing industries. Their owners, who abandoned the city in haste (6th century A.D.) either when the city was sacked by the Arabs or because of natural calamity, must have buried these objects. This collection of utilitarian items is invaluable, since it is the only one representing the early historical period of Saurashtra. The indented coast also provided for convenient exchanges amongst the ships entering the Arabian Sea during this period as evident from the discovery of a number of Amphoras and Indo-Greek coins.

Coins, Seals and Sealing

The coin deposits found in a regular sequence at Hathab have greatly helped in dating the structural remains. The numismatic evidence is further corelated by ceramic and paleographic evidences, besides a hoard of coins from the moat which is yet to be studied as the coins

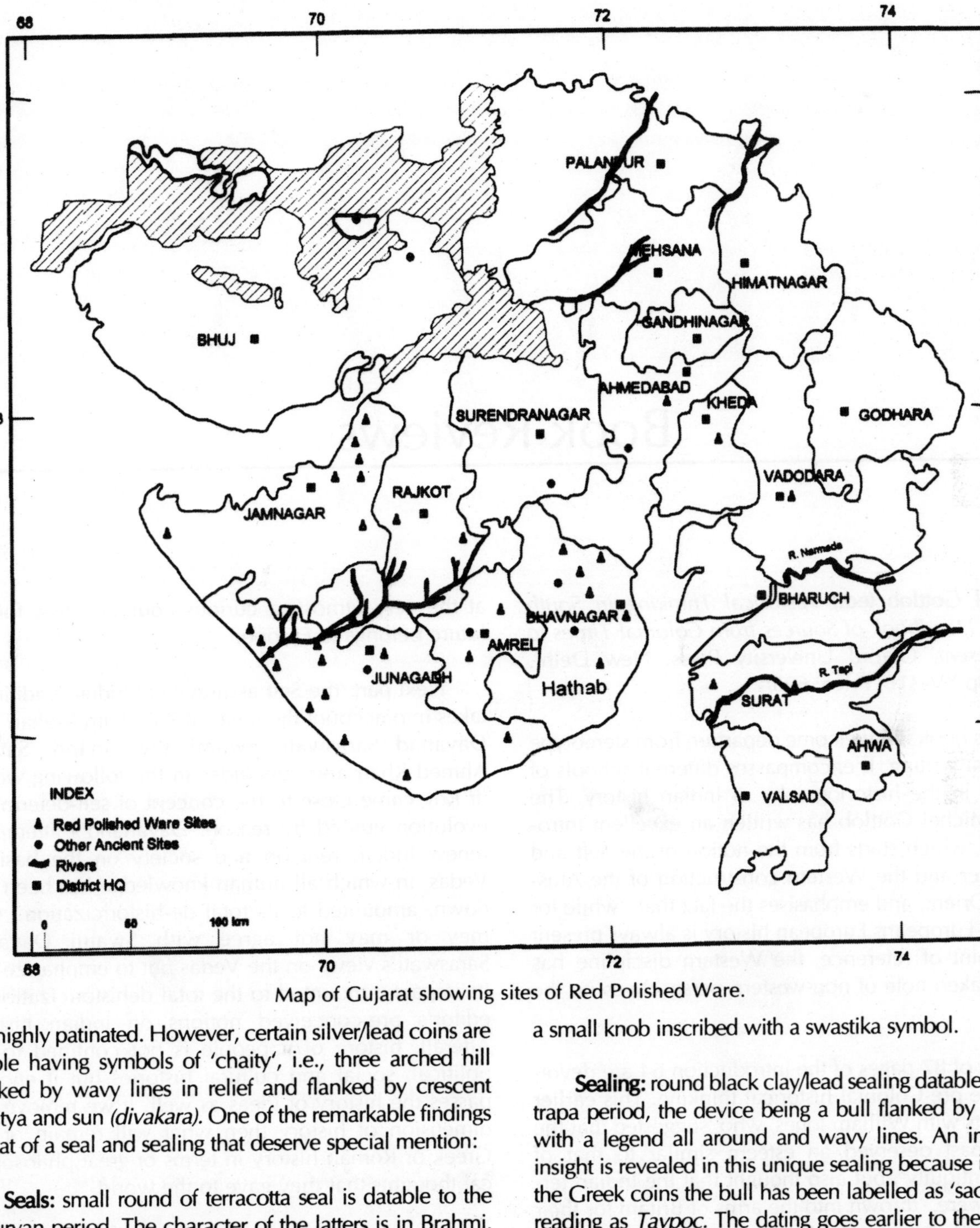

Map of Gujarat showing sites of Red Polished Ware.

are highly patinated. However, certain silver/lead coins are visible having symbols of 'chaity', i.e., three arched hill marked by wavy lines in relief and flanked by crescent chaitya and sun *(divakara).* One of the remarkable findings is that of a seal and sealing that deserve special mention:

Seals: small round of terracotta seal is datable to the Mauryan period. The character of the latters is in Brahmi. The legend's reading is as *Abadavo,* the reverse part having a small knob inscribed with a swastika symbol.

Sealing: round black clay/lead sealing datable to Kshatrapa period, the device being a bull flanked by *stambha* with a legend all around and wavy lines. An interesting insight is revealed in this unique sealing because in one of the Greek coins the bull has been labelled as 'sacred bull' reading as *Taypoc.* The dating goes earlier to the 1st century B.C. Apart from these mould have also been found.

Book Reviews

Michael Gottlob (ed.) *Historical Thinking in South Asia: A Handbook of Sources from Colonial Times to the Present,* Oxford University Press, New Delhi, 2003, pp.XV-318. Price: 695/-

This book is a welcome departure from stereotype historical writing. It encompasses different schools of thought in the historiography of Indian history. The editor Michel Gottlob has written an excellent introduction, which starts from the notion of the Self and the Other and the Western construction of the Ahistorical Orient, and emphasises the fact that, 'while for the non-Europeans European history is always present as a point of reference, the Western discipline has hardly taken note of non-western perspectives on the world'.

Out of 87 pages of the introduction 64 are devoted to the pre-Colonial historical thinking. This earlier part starts with William Jones, who 'suggested that the Indian past deserved an esteem similar to that of Greek antiquity', but also thought that the Indian territories were, 'thrown into the arms of Britain for their protection'. After presenting the main hypothesis of James Mill, Hegel, Marx, Macaulay, it comes to Max Muller for whom India was not a 'distant, strange, or, at the very utmost, a curious country. India for the future belongs to Europe.'

Next part 'the Self assurance of Indian traditions, takes into account the ideas of Raja Ram Mohan Roy, Dayanad Saraswati, Swami Vivekanand, Sayyed Ahmed Khan and concludes in the following words, 'If Roy came close to the concept of self-determined evolution guided by reason, Dayanand's attempt to renew Indian religion and society on the basis of Vedas, in which all human knowledge has been laid down, amounted to its total de-historicization.' One may or may not agree with Swami Dayanad Saraswati's views on the Vedas but to emphasize that its impact 'amounted to the total dehistoricization' is editor's pre-conceived notions on Indian history. Afterall, history of a people is not confined to the political, social and cultural histories but it encompasses the history of ideas as well. If we remove this dimension of history then what will remain of the Greek or Roman history in terms of great philosophical thoughts that they gave to the world.

This book is valuable as it includes translation of writings of Bakim Chandra Chatterji and Nirmal Verma for the first time in English language. Some of the questions raised by Bakim Chandra in 1882-83 seem relevant even today, 'How long has Europe been Civilized? 400 years back, in 15th century, Europe was even more uncivilized than us. By stroke of one incident Europe became civilized. All of sudden Europe got back the perished, forgotten own Greek literature. Like a thin stream that swelled by the rain water and inundate its banks, or a dying patient gets back his youthful strength after taking a miraculous medicine, Europe suddenly flourished.' This upholds the reviewer's point of view noted above.

The similar questions were also raised in the 19th century by the pioneers of Reform Movement. Gottlob's assessment of their views is revealing:' The Hindu reform movements emphasize, it is true, the dynamic elements of Indian culture, but these tendencies towards essentialism rendered it difficult to conceive meaningful processes of change. The result is not historicization of the relation between the cultures but a hierarchical subordination of the Other below the Self.' This viewpoint presupposes that the tendencies of essentialism are opposed to progress or change. It is true that Indian historians have remained obsessed with the Other, particularly Europe, as is evident from the fact that most of the Indian Universities still have European history as a compulsory subject in their syllabus, but to the editor the ides of the Other being below the Self in Indian context is too troublesome. Here, because of the Euro-centric views which is hardly valid now even though it had the full play during the colonial period in India when the ICS masters had to be told the superiority of the West over the East so that the East will always feel small before the West and accept their rule, many authors keep on repeating it in one way or the other, including science and technology This was, incidentally, also the view of Karl Marx when he wrote near two dozen articles on India in the 19th century in which he emphasised the superiority of Europe over India.

'Pre-colonial historical thinking' includes the writers of Indian languages like Shiv Prashad who wrote *Timirnsaka* in 1864 and Bharatendu Harishchandra who has been referred to as 'Harischandra of Banaras' but to the Indian mind and memory he will always remain Bharatendu Hasrishchandra. According to Gottlob '(Bharatendu) Harishchandra sought to prove the existence of things in ancient India which today are considered to be modern and above which the foreigners boasted, calling them their own, deplored, 'the flow of wealth to a foreign land,' and long before the Swadeshi agitations of the early 20th century, he requested that the Indians buy only goods manufactured in their own country.'

This section of introduction ends with the thinking of Gandhi 'who revealing more historical consciousness than revivalists and admirers of ancient Indian greatness, he stated; 'if we have to make progress we must not repeat history but make new history. We must add to the inheritance left by our ancestors.'

The later part of the Introduction highlights the historical thinking in the contemporary South Asia and starts with R. C. Majumdar who, in his Presidential Address, at the 6th Annual Conference of the Institute of Historical Studies at Srinagar in 1968, expressed his concerns. 'Certain new trends are growing among the section of Indian historians which violet the high ideas of truth,' and then comes to Romila Thapar who according to the editor 'concerned herself with the 'Past and Prejudice' and confronts some of the assumptions which were at the centre of the Nationalist as well as the western Colonist view of Indian history with new results of research', and further adds 'while examining the conventional concepts in the light of new evidence, Thapar also occupied herself with widespread ideas about the lack of historical thinking in India.' Here again the author shows his bias against the traditional Indian views of history.

Gottlob writes about Romila Thapar and Devahuti in the same paragraph and shows the contrast in their thinking in the following words, 'Thapar did not question, however, the universality of the methodological standards. The enlightening potential of the scientific approach to history should rather be used in the interest of Indian Self-determination. In contrast to this in the late 1970s a group of historians who sought to bring to the fore the specifically Indian features of history, questioned the suitability of western categories and even of comparative approaches for the interpretation of Indian past. The Indian History and Culture Society (IHCS) focussed the attention of scholars on questions of value judgements, national identity, etc., and also criticised the use of non-Indian concepts like 'slave-owning society' 'Asiatic Mode of Production', etc.' The new association of historians, according to its president Devhuti, ultimately aimed at 'Indian framework of interpretation' for the Indian past; for 'the general becomes intelligible only through the specific, the universal through the unique'. The general concepts were to be gained from one's own experience. Historians with an orientation towards progress were, in particular the Marxist, countered by Devahuti'; 'we have to be our own 'messiahs', to feel, to understand, to interpret our own history'.

The above statement paints Devhuti's thinking as anti-progress because she countered those historians who had orientation towards 'progress', particularly the Marxist. Devhuti's search for Indian framework has been quoted in these words, 'the Indian historians interest should be directed towards, 'what the Indian people, ordinary or special thought and said about events and ideas,' even if this meant the conversion of history into myths and symbols'. This critique although subtle, clearly misrepresents Devhuti and Indian History and Culture Society. Gottlob completely failed to understand the aims and objectives of IHCS, as expressed in Devhuti's writings, or else he deliberately twists them. Devhuti never sought to convert history into myths and symbols in her insistence that Puranas can also be used as a source of history. Afterall serious scholars of Ancient Indian History, including the Westerners, like A.L.Basham, and now Romila Thapar too, have culled out 'history' out of myths and legends. Have the Europeans not did the same when they took up what is called 'Holyland Archaeology'. Have they not tried to see in the Biblical stories the 'history' of their own nation? For the truthful history of a people no foreign framework, grounds even on methodological grounds can work. There should be a common yardstick to judge the history of all Nationalist since the history of each nation is a unique product of its own people.

The views of R. C. Majumdar and Tarachand are also compared in the following words, 'initially, Majumdar had been chosen to write the history of Freedom Movement in India, but his draft which deviated in some essential points from the government lines was passed over. 'While Tarachand laid stress upon evidence of communal harmony, Majumdar emphasized the evidence of Hindu-Muslim conflict as being a constant feature of Indian history.' But the fact is that truth lies neither in only conflict nor only in harmony, both were integral parts of our history. And this is true of the histories of all the people all over the world.

Among contemporary historians R. S. Sharma's theory of feudalism is discussed and is contradicted by Ashok Rudra in the following words, 'to perceive the Indian social order as a form of feudalism seemed to Ashok Rudra like trying to explain European society by referring to the Indian caste system.' Irfan Habib, Harbans Mukhia and several others also had criticized R. S. Sharma's theory on Indian feudalism. In fact, every serious scholar had something or the other to say against his theory.

The detailed and insightful Introduction ends with the most recent Subaltern Studies, feminist historiography and environmental history. According to Gottlob, 'in contrast to earlier Marxist approaches, however, one of the outstanding features of the projects (Subaltern Studies) is its avoidance of concept of totality, which expropriate the Subaltern of his specific experience in the name of the evolution of the whole', and 'in the wake of Subaltern Studies historical research in India has (re) discovered other remote areas; regional and local traditions, the self-consciousness of the Dalits, the tribal identities, gender roles, etc.'

The truth is, however, that pieces are important to construct the whole but over- emphasis on pieces and parts as the scholars of the Subaltern Studies Project have been doing, is repeating the same mistake which Marxist historians have been making in viewing the

Indian history through Marx's framework. Indian history can neither be written nor explained or conceived on the basis of borrowed tools. This leads to partial truth only. Parts do not make the whole, the whole contains parts and yet it is much more than the individual parts.

One has, however, to agree with R. S. Sharma's viewpoint that 'ancient India should not be confused with Hindu India or Medieval India.' The question of periodization of Indian history has again to be faced squarely. Is it necessary to cut the flow of history in periods? American history never needed such periodization as it never had 'ancient' or 'medieval' period. Only Europeans had middle ages, so our search of medieval period and it boundaries in Indian history, leads us to a blind ally. Do we have to always move in circles? Can't we, for once, come out of it and see ourselves?'

This book of sources provides some answer to above question in the thinking of Nirmal Verma. As this extract has been published for the first time in English it will be worth quoting in detail:

'In spite of external changes the basic flow of Indian life didn't udergo any major change. The way in which we always looked at reality, the way we associated ourselves with time and nature, our attitude towards death, from which one can construe our view of life- all these have not changed basically, even in the course of time only the external reality has changed.(′.)

If the Indian consciousness has remained relatively untouched by the changes, it does not mean that history has not exercised its incessant pressure on it. On the one hand, the dark mythical roots of our consciousness which had remained unhurt were run over by the water of historical reality, and, on the other hand, we had to also make compromise with the constantly changing historical reality at the practical level. In fact, the Indian 'character' was formed between these two extremes; accepting history at the practical level and totally ignoring its pressure on the mental level- in this dualistic process we have succeeded in creating an unusual balance; because only in this balance we could retain alive our basic identity.'

The second part of the book from which the above portion is quoted is as important as the Introduction. Here one gets to read almost all the shades of interpretation of Indian history in one book. Coming from the pen of an author of European origin, the book establishes two facts. One, Indian historiography lacks one single work which gives the whole picture based on equal emphasis on literary, epigraphic, numismatic, archaeological and regional sources and can take into account the social, cultural, political and economic, all aspects of life of any single period. But if Michael Gottlob can do it in historiographical context, surely Indian scholars can be inspired to do it in historical context too. Secondly, Indian historians need to look back at themselves from a little distance. Either we have remained over-obsessed with the 'Other' or with the 'Self'.

The balance has been hinted by scholars like Nirmal Verma. This volume brings with surgical precision the historiography without being over-judgemental, even though at many places Europan as well as Marxist bias is more than subtle.

The extensive bibliography given at the end also enhances the value of this book. Barring few omissions, such as K. M. Panikar's book published in 1953 has been quoted in the text but is missing in the bibliography, this book is certainly a 'must' for all serious scholars of Indian history as a handbook of sources from the Colonial period to the Present.

Vandana Kaushik

Zahiruddin Malik *Agrarian System in Medieval India (Land Revenue Arrangement in Sarkar Shahabad* (Bihar), 1734-1790, Centre of Advanced Study in History, Aligarh, 2001, p.207. Price: Rs.395/-

The subject of agrarian system in Medieval India is of absorbing interest. Though several books have been written on it by eminent scholars, based on deep researches during the last years, many of its aspects still remain controversial. The author has given here an account of the agrarian system which existed in Shahabad during 1734-1790. This study, based on the recently discovered contemporary source material, mainly document containing statistical data, both in Persian and English, examines those elements that formed the land revenue structure designed for a *'pargana'* under the Mughal's and the changes effected in its working by the British *'sarkar'* in Shahabad, Suba Bihar, during 1734-1790. The Book is worth reading for those scholars who want to have knowledge of the agrarian system of the Medieval period in India; and what impact it had on the zamindars and the peasants. It also helps to know the various policies and measures pursued by the British to obtain maximum land revenue and reviews their adverse effects in the region particularly in Shahabad. Also, that the economic policy of the state was not calculated to ensure the economic prosperity of the people.

Anita Khatri

Anup Taneja (ed.) *Sufi Cults and the Evolution of the Medieval Indian Culture*, Indian Council of Historical Research, 2003, pp.viii+328. Price: Rs. 950

Indian Council of Historical research has so far published eight monographs under the Monograph Series, to provide fresh interpretations and explorations into unknown or lesser known fields of history. The present work, Monograph no.9, is the latest in this series. It presents the various facets of the evolution and spread of the Sufi influence in India and a critical evaluation of the role played by the Sufi saints for the establishment of a pluralist society in India.

It contains scholarly presentations on various themes like emergence of Sufi *silsilas* and Sufi cults in India, their similarities with other non-Muslim mystical traditions, their interactions with the non-Muslim environment and their attitude towards State and orthodox *ulama* and Sufi perception of women in the 16th century patriarchal society.

Fatima Hussain in her essay entitled 'Emergence of Sufi *Silsilas* in India' says that Sufism is a distinctive way of life, which did not come into being immediately after Prophet Mohammad. It emerged and evolved slowly. It was only during the Sultanate period that the Sufi ideology began to take an organised shape in the form *silsilas.* Then she discusses the evolution of Sufism as has been defined by J.S. Terimingham into these distinct phases- the *khanquah* was some sort of school where the wandering Sufis could practice spirituality under the informal guidance of some master. The striking feature of *tariqa* stage was the systematisation of various mystical techniques and practices. As compared to the *khanqah* phase where the Sufis were undifferentiated at the social level the *tariqa* phase was characterised by differentiated schools of discipline. The Sufis were now officiated to one *silsila* or the other. The conspicuous feature of the *tai'fa* phase was the elevation of the *Pir* to the stature of a living deity, who was an object of adoration and worship by the Murids. Though she says that some saints contributed a great deal to promoting communal harmony and inculcating high spiritual and moral values among the masses but this aspect has not been elaborated. Iqtidar Husain Siddiqui in his essay, 'Sufi Cults and the Making of a Pluralist Society' emphasises the social role played by Sufis. He says the magnanimity and tolerant attitude of Sufis towards people, irrespective of birth or creed, paved the way for interaction between the followers of different religious traditions. They were the pioneers in starting inter-religious dialogue for communal harmony and peace among the followers of different religions, particularly Islam and Hinduism. He has discussed the influence of Brahmanism, Buddhism, Shamanism and Hindu yogis on Sufi cults.

I. A. Zilli in his essay, 'Early Chistis and the State', attempts to examine the Chisti attitude towards the state afresh. He says the Chistis are considered to have cut themselves off completely from kings and courts. They are said to have avoided all kinds of association with kings, politics and government service. However, a critical perusal of the evidence does not seem to fully support this view. Some of the disciples of Nizam-ud-Din Auliya did occupy important positions in the government during the Sultanate period. He says Sultan Muhammad bin Tughlaq was not ill-disposed against the Chistis as is generally believed.

The hitherto neglected parts of Sufism has been exposed by Raziuddin Aquil in his essay, 'Miracles, Authority and Benevolence: Stories of Karamat in Sufi Literature of the Delhi Sultanate.' He discusses the manner in which miracles created conditions in establishing the authority of the Sufis on a firm footing in the society. He says miracles served as a weapon to overawe, subdue, terrorise and occasionally even to annihilate the opponents.

Mohammad Ishaq Khan in his essay, 'Sharia, State and Conversions in the Medieval Kashmir: An Assessment of Mir Sayyid Ali Hamadani's Historical Role' has critically examined the source material available on the entrance of Islam into the Kashmir valley. According to Khan, Mir Sayyid Ali pointed to the *Ulama's* failure in captivating the hearts of non-Muslims by the nobility of their actions. In contrast, he exalts the true Brahmin and his idol. Mir Sayyid Ali did not stand for radical Islamisation of Kashmir society as has been generally believed but to make ruler sheave the universalist aims of the *din* (faith) namely, moral and social uplift of mankind through spiritual guidance and philanthropology. S. K. Abdul Latif in his essay entitled, ' Shaikh Jalal-ud-din Tabrezi and his contribution to the spread of Sufi influence in Bengal during the thirteenth century.' Has analysed the role of Shaikh from a Sanskrit work entitled Seka Subhodaya in his essay, 'The Pro-Alien Policy of Ahmed Shah and the Role of the Bahmani Kingdom set into motion a new trend which proved instrumental in the establishment of three shi'i states, the growth of shi'ism and opening of the doors of diplomacy between sh'i Persia and the Deccan the *safavid* Persia and the Deccan.

Main concern of Geeta Arya in her essay, 'Woman in Malik Muhammad Jaisi's Discourse: Padmavat, Akhrawat and Akhiri Kalam' is to reconstruct the history of women during the medieval period. She says according to Jayqi's writings in the 16th century north India, women of both the upper and lower sections were regarded as subordinate to men.

S. M. Azizuddin Husain in his essay, 'Sufi Cults and the Shias' on the basis of the works of Shia *ulama* on *tasawwuf,* says that there was no contradiction between shi'i beliefs and Sufi practices. Kumkum Srivastav has explored in detail the *qalandriyya* part in her essay entitled, 'The qalandars and the *qalandariyya* Path (*tariqa*)', she says it was the name of an antinomian sect of Sufis and a not-so-strictly organised Sufi *tariqa*. Historians of Sufism agree that the term *qalandar* is much older than the institutionalisation of the 'path' of *qalandars* emerged as a separate and identifiable group. They formed an anti thesis of the Khanqah or settled Sufis.

Thus, the present work focuses on the role played by Sufi saints in medieval India in creating a congenial environment where people of different sects could interact with each other in more healthy manner and how it helped in the development of a composite culture.

Anita Gupta

J.N. Agrawal *Inscriptions of Haryana, Himachal Pradesh, Punjab, Kashmir and Adjoining Hilly Tracts,* ICHR and Pratibha Prakashan, Delhi, 1999, pp xxiii-462, plates 95. Price: Rs. 1180/-

The author has put in an in-depth efforts in studying the inscriptions of Haryana, Himachal Pradesh, Punjab, Jammu & Kashmir and the adjoining hill tracts from C. A.D. 600 to 1500.

Various controversies have been put to rest with the proper reading of the inscriptions. The author gives a detailed introduction which critically examines political, historical and other aspects related to the socio-economic and religious life. The entire text and corresponding translations have been done anew and are given region wise. The volume is accompanied with coloured plates for the benefit of readers.

It is a systematic study of the inscriptions of the period from AD 600-1500 and will be of immense help to researchers and epigraphists.

Sonali Gupta

Aruna Tripathi, *The Buddhist Art of Kauśambi, Emerging Perceptions in Buddhist Studies,* No. 17, D.K Printworld (p) Ltd., New Delhi, 2003, pp xxii-342, Maps 2, b/w photos 322, col. Illustrations 54 Price: Rs. 2500/-

The monograph which is first on the subject, is an attempt to highlight the importance of the stone sculptures of Kausambi. The author's systematic and analytical approach is first of its kind and has done justice to what Kausambi is rightly worthy of. The most important aspect of the work is the nature of its source-material.

The work deals in particular with Buddhist Art from 300 B.C., i.e, from Mauryan the finding of sculptures is from the regular excavations carried out by the Allahabad University under Prof. G.R. Sharma. Hence , the data is authentic and from context to the Gupta period, 500 A.D. Also, the evolution of Buddhist Art with reference to technical aspects of plastic art.

Providing readers with a backdrop of what was Kausambi, the author explores in brief its history with the help of literary as well as archaeological sources. She goes on to elucidate on the traditions of Buddhism which highlighted the role of Kausambi.

Chapter four discusses in detail the archaeological excavations and explorations made till date at Kausambi and its vicinity. After having formed a base, the author builds on the specificity of the sculptures and makes an attempt to document it period wise with the aid of coloured visuals. It is a complete catalogue, written precisely and in lucid language.

In Chapter six, the author gives a critical view of Buddhist Art of Kausambi. The next chapter deals with the types and techniques in stone working. The author culminates the discussion with summary and conclusion, wherein she refrains from branding the sculptures to be exclusively from the Kausambi School as, according to her, it would be inconclusive to speak of an entire school. In any case, her area of study is confined as of now only to the Buddhist sculptures.

It is an impressive and commendable attempt made by the author and, therefore, recommended strongly. The book has been beautifully produced and is a model of publication.

K.S. Ramachandran

Vijay Kumar *Ancient Indian Society: Continuity and Change,* Sanjay Prakashan, Delhi. 2002,pp.258. Price Rs. 495/-

This book is the Ph.D. thesis of Dr. Vijay Kumar. It deals with the different aspects of society viz. varnasrama dharma, position of women, rules regarding marriage, widowhood, purdah, etc. and the changes that took place from the Rigvedic times to 1200A.D.

The book is divided into seven chapters. In the first chapter, the author discusses what is meant by social change and how time, space, place and human needs play an important part in the formation of dharma (duty). The changes in the society have been described from historical point of view from Rigvedic period to the later Vedic period. The discussion is with regard to the disintegration of the joint family, the preference for the son, marriageable age of the girls, the important role played by the iron and its impact on the economy and society of the period.

In the second chapter 'Challenges and Social Changes-1st phase of Kali Age' the author has concluded 'that mostly social changes occur due to political and economic factors but sometimes developments in religious spheres also assume an important role'. The author refers to the occurrence of deterioration in the social order due to Kali Age in which dharma was on the verge of complete decline. This chapter also throws light on the different features of Kali Age such as the growing importance of wealth which became the source of acquiring high family status.

While agreeing with Dr. R.S. Sharma, Dr. Vijay Kumar in the third chapter 'Challenges as Determining Factors-2nd phase of Kali Age', gives information that political vacuum created by the downfall of Kushanas in the North and Satvahanas in the South and decline of long distance trade with the Romans, Chinese and Parthians were contributory factors for the urban decay and this loss of economy led to a social crisis. The migrations from towns to villages willingly or forced by the political upheaval also determined the social changes. The author discusses in detail the role of politics and various religions such as Brahmanism, Buddhism, Jainism, Tantricism, Shaivism in bringing the social changes. This chapter deals with the changes that took place during the post- Gupta and early medieval period.

In the fourth chapter it is stated that the continuous decline in economic conditions of the brahmins made the law-givers to popularise *dana* by writing treatises on that-hence the *danakanda* of *Krtyakalpataru,* Vallalseana's *Danasagara,* etc. The role played by religion can be seen where conversions to heterodox sects led to taking up of different professions. Here, one sees the upward mobility in the *Kali Yuga* i.e. the upper caste people were forced to take the professions of lower castes and lower castes could take to the professions of higher castes which otherwise generally denied by the ancient law-givers. According to the author, the changes took place in every institution and aspect of life i.e. not only in all the four castes but in all the four *ashramas* and *purusharathas* as well.

The fifth chapter deals with the changes in institutions such as family, marriage, position of women, education, etc. The economic changes, pressures of foreigners and the life style of people affected these institutions. The urbanisation led to weakening of joint family system. 'Changes that occurred in various institutions modified the traditional social order and its mechanism' (p.151). The higher castes were no more privileged class whereas lower caste improved their social and economic status.

In the chapter six, the author discusses the significant steps taken by the law givers to restrict the movements and changes to restore the brahmanical order as these changes did not favour the privileged classes of the brahmanical social order. To bring back the order the theory of incarnations and formations of the doctrine of *Kalivarja* (actions forbidden in the Kali age) were their most important efforts in this regard. This also included the concept of *dana-dakshina* and visit to the holy places *(tirtha).*

The Chapter seven gives the conclusion of the author. Its states that various institutions of Indian society kept on changing in their nature and scope in an evolutionary process.

This book presents the information in a lucid style. A comprehensive bibliography of primary and secondary sources enhances the importance of the work. The references at the end of each chapter establish the depth of the research work done by the author.

Saroj Gulati

Aparna Basu and Anup Taneja (ed.) *Breaking Out of Invisibility- Woman in Indian History,* Indian Council of Historical Research, 2003, pp.viii+343. Price: Rs.650/-

This volume contains fourteen essays on various themes of women studies. All the essays can be divided in various categories. Some reflect the gender perspectives in time-frame of history such as Kumkum Roy's *'Investigating Gendered Religious Traditions'.* It presents a survey of post 1990 studies in the field of religious traditions particularly Jain, Buddhist and

Vedic. She starts with Padmanabh Jaini's *'Gender and Salvation'* published in 1991 and ends with Vijay Ramaswamy's *'Walking Naked: Women, Society, Spirituality in South India'* published in 1997. It presents a critical survey of major works on women in religious traditions. Ranjana Sheel's *'Brahmanising' State, 'Sanskritising' Castes and Dowry* in Colonial India' and Lata Singh's *'Gender Nationalism and Khadi: Rendering Woman as Domestic (ated) and not Political Subjects'*, can be put in the same category as they relate to the time-frame of colonial India.

Shalini Shah and Devika Rangachari have analysed gender issues on the basis of the *Mahabharta* and *Rajatarangini* to illustrate the genderising of political processes in Punjab and Kashmir respectively. Meera Kosambi gives a graphic picture of Anandibai Karve's life In Maharashtra. She focuses on Anandibai's role in the social history of Maharashtra and her unclaimed contribution to the success of social reforms. This essay candidly portraits the dilemma of Maharshi Karve, who often having proved his reformist credentials by marrying a widow, at last succumbed to the public pressure and marginalised Anandibai in his own reformist activities. Rajul Sogani has also dealt with the theme of widow-remarriage. She has based her thesis on the Indian fiction between 1857-1930. Gujrati, Bengali, Marathi, Hindi and Urdu novels of this period reflect the prejudice against widow remarriage among the high caste Hindus although the Widow Remarriage Act was passed in 1856.

Ranjana Sheel has analysed the custom of dowry among the Hindu Society and has traced its origin to the *'Negative Impact of Socio-Political and Economic Forces Unleashed by the Colonial State'* but dowry is not a colonial evil, it was prevalent even in medieval times also and we have references from the Persian sources of 14th century that Muslim Sultan gave money as charity for the dowry of poor Muslim girls. Partna Chatterji's thesis is that in the development of nationalist movement, women were projected as mothers or goddesses which served to erase her sexuality so that she could participate in the nationalist movement without losing her social respectability.

Vijay Ramaswamy has emphasised on the Tamil quest for identity and self-expression and the role of women in the Tamil Ethno-nationalist Movement. According to Ramswamy the Tani Tamizh Iyakkan tried to resist the onslaught on their culture from English colonialism from outside and Hindi colonialism from within. This essay also illustrates the urge to silence women's voices in Tamil society.

Karin Deutsch Karlekar has analysed the views of Muslim spokesmen in the period 1914-38 and she thinks that 'Muslim woman during this period ceased to be a passive recipients of reform processes and were actively defining and discussing issues of concern to themselves as Muslim women. She concludes that 'Islamic Personal Law' has not always been keen as scared site or essential part of Indian Muslim's distinctive identity, but was constructed as such during the late colonial period; and they (Muslim women) were more concerned with establishing their rights as women.'

Pratima Kamat has given a critique of the institutions of charity the *recolhimentos* in the Golden Goa city space. According to her they were instrument of colonisations. These institutions were established with apparent objective of providing help to destitute widows, orphan girls and concerned themselves almost exclusively with the welfare of the European ladies living in Goa. The society in the 16th and 17th century Goa was heaven for the disgraceful and licentious activities of the rich. Adultery, rape, murders of wives were rampant. Thus to provide shelter to the widows, destitute wives and orphan girls *recolhimentos* were established. These orphan girls were sent from Portugal to be married and settled in Goa. These orphans and the institutions of charity both were instruments of colonisation.

Thus, this volume has brought several scholars working on gender issues on one platform and it will be a useful tool for the researchers of this field. It has an excellent introduction by the editors which not only gives an insight into the essays of the volumes but also provides a solid background. The annotated bibliography on gender studies is another useful part of the book which can be used as a ready reference. Indian Council of Historical Research has done a commendable job in publishing this monograph series and this particular volume has the scholarly imprint of Aparna Basu the editor.

Vandana Kaushik

S.K Bhatt, 'The Art and Architecture of Mandu', *The Journal of Academy of Indian Numismatics and Sigillography,* vol. XVI Indore, 2002, pp xxx- 99, plates 14. Price: Rs. 400/-

The present work is a welcome attempt in unveiling the treasures of the Mandu School of Paintings. The author not only focuses on the splendid architecture of Mandu but also places its importance in the world of paintings. The paintings not only show the beauty of the paintings but also the depth with which a subject has been treated. The book includes coloured illustrations which is a visual treat.

The work fills in the blanks in the field of Art History and brings the Mandu School into focus.

Sonali Gupta

Krishan, Yuvraj *Understanding Partition (India Sundered: Muslims Fragmented),* Bhartiya Vidya Bhawan, Mumbai, 2002, pp. xiii + 520. Price Rs. 300/-

The book under review analyses objectively, different events leading to the partition of the country, into two independent countries, India and Pakistan. However, it does not deal with a related subject, India's freedom movement and the withdrawal of the British. The sole aim of the work is to understand the immediate causes of the Partition including the historical roots of the ideology of separatism which found expression in the two-nation theory.

Though the creation of Pakistan was a triumph of the two-nation theory, yet, the author asserts that it was a tragedy for the Indian Muslims for whom the homeland of Pakistan was established. He adds that Jinnah and the Muslim League never wanted to realise that a mere division of the country could not have made it possible for Muslims of the provinces in which they were in minority, to escape the inevitable political domination of the Hindus in a democratic set up. On the other hand, the Muslims of the majority provinces did not need partition, to save them from the Hindu *'raj'*. Thus, the establishment of Pakistan has failed to solve the problem it was intended to resolve.

The author has thoroughly scrutinised the facts and views of the historians and others, and found it absolutely wrong that Nehru's refusal to accommodate Muslim's League's desire to share power in the United Provinces in 1937, with the Congress Party, was responsible for pushing the League to the goal of Pakistan. Similarly, it is erroneous to accuse the Congress leadership ' Nehru, Patel, and Rajendra Prasad ' of throwing away the last chance of maintaining a united India by rejecting the Cabinet Mission Plan of 1946. On the other hand, the author argues that the Plan, as drawn up by the Cabinet Mission, would have balkanised the country and eventually led to the formation of a 'bigger Pakistan'. It was, therefore, the author says, the supreme act of statesmanship of the Congress leaders which outmanoeuvred Jinnah (and Wavell) as the whole of the undivided Punjab, Bengal, and Assam would have then gone in the formation of Pakistan.

Pakistan was the creation primarily of Jinnah. In this endeavour, he was aided by the rulers who enabled him to liquidate alternative, non-communal leadership of the nationalist and other Muslims, by treating the Muslim League as the sole representative of the Muslims of India.

Role of Lord Mountbatten has also been analysed. Thus, by advancing the date of transfer of power from June 1948 to August 1947, he had brought a breakdown of the administrative machinery. Nearly, 10 million people migrated to each side of the Indo-Pakistan border, and about 2 millions lost their lives, mainly because the time period for a peaceful transfer of population was too short.

Another dimension of the Partition, is that those Muslim League leaders, who were staunch believers in the two-nation theory and who worked for the establishment of Pakistan, did not migrate but stayed back in India, and joined the Congress Party which they had opposed before the Partition. They came to occupy important offices in the Party, and in the Central and State Governments. Likewise, *Ulemas* and *madrassas,* and *Pirs* of *dargahs,* who supported the division of the country, also did not shift out of India. The specific instance of the Aligarh Muslim University which played an active role in formulating the ideology of separatism and in mobilising Muslims to support the ideal of Pakistan, have continued to be the centre of Muslim separatism and a champion of an 'oppressed and persecuted community' in secular India. Hence, the author concludes that the Partition has failed to solve the problems of Hindu-Muslim conflict.

The author also examines the specific allegations of the Muslim League regarding atrocities on the Muslims during the Congress rule in the provinces during 1937-39 and concludes that they were all baseless. Even the British in authority were also of the same view-point. Thus, the author observes that the Partition has created two States which have been perpetually in a state of conflict.

The book includes several documents in original, as appendices. They increase the value of the work. Though many primary sources have been extensively used, a number of secondary sources have also been referred to. It would have increased the value of the book if the author had consulted the primary sources wherever required and employ the secondary sources only when analysis and interpretations were needed. The Debates of the Central Assembly, though constituting an important primary source, have not been used. Likewise, Dr. Ram Manohar Lohia's book on the similar subject has not been consulted.

The book though written in lucid style, contains typographical mistakes at several places. The language is simple and readability is quite high. The book projects views and analysis which are quite different from the same in other books on similar subjects. This would be a good addition in any collection on Modern Indian History.

D.K. Kaushik

Snigdha Tripathy, *Inscriptions of Orissa (Inscriptions of Bhauma-Karas)* vol II, ICHR and Pratibha Prakashan, Delhi, 1999, plates 19, Price: Rs. 750/-

The ICHR embarked on the "Inscriptions of India' venture in the 1970's. The present author came out with her "Inscriptions of Orissa" Vol.1 which covered the fifth to the eighth centuries AD. The present volume, second in line, on inscriptions of Orissa concentrates on the inscriptions of the Bhauma-Kara dynasty who were in power from the eighth to the tenth century A.D.

The author has studied the inscriptions from the first hand sources which include original copper plates and stone records. Inscriptions numbering to 26 have been studied, however the ones issued by the feudatories have been excluded.

The work is divided into two parts. The first half gives the detailed introduction relating to the history of the Bhauma-Karas and the socio-economic and cultural history of that period on the basis of epigraphic sources. The second half is devoted to the texts of the inscriptions which are shown verbatum followed by an explanation of the contents in English.

It is a praiseworthy effort and is recommended for scholars interested in the subject.

Sonali Gupta

Shashikant *The Hathigumpha Inscription of Kharavela and the Bhābru Edict of Aśoka,* D.K Printworld (p) Ltd., New Delhi, 2000, pp xxiv-168, b/w photos 19, Maps 2. Price: Rs. 295/-

The famous Hathigumpha inscription and Bhabru Edict of Asoka are the windows to the then age. The Hathigumpha inscription unveils the social, political and cultural conditions of the three centuries before Christ's birth. The author gives an introduction along with the history of its decipherment, the site and the text of the inscriptions. He elaborates on the probable date of the inscription and its author as well. Its significance in confirming to traditions of the Jaina world is brought forth. The author's translation is a welcome step towards a deeper understanding of this historical document.

Likewise, the Bhabru Edict of Asoka, a record of Buddhist scripture and monastic organisation is also well explained. A separate section is devoted to the genesis of the *Prakrit* languages and the tradition of scripts and writing in Ancient India.

The author delves deep into these inscriptions bringing out their historicity and thematic similarity. It is an earnest attempt to interpret the documents keeping their context in view. New theories have also been propounded which are based on latest archaeological finds. The work is well illustrated with photographs and transcription charts.

Now in its second enlarged edition, it is highly recommended for epigraphists, historians and researchers who will stand to gain from this work.

Anuja Geetali

Amrendra Kumar Singh, *Temples of the Kalachuri Period,* Pratibha Prakashan, Delhi, 2002, pp xvi+118, drawings 16, Illustrations 90. Price: Rs. 1650/-

The present work speaks of the development of architecture in the Kalachuri Period in Central India. Temples in the vicinity have also been taken into account for a better perspective.

The author begins by placing the Kalachuris in the historical perspectives and also gives their architecture an overview by elaborating on their horizontal and vertical plans. The author then focuses on the temples of architectural and sculptural importance discussing their plans in detail. From the monolithic type to the structural temples, the author is successful in discerning the gradual process of evolution in this region. The work is well illustrated with drawings and photographs. It will prove to be a benefit to those interested in the Indian architecture.

Sonali Gupta

Shrimati Pankaj Ameta *Malwa Ke Parmara Shaskon Ki Rajasva Vyavastha,* (in Hindi) Academy of Indian Numismatics and Sigilography, Indore, 2001. pp.147+Bibliography + 32 plates+pp. 7 introduction etc. Price Rs.300/-

The authors of repute have already written books on the Paramaras such as *Parmara Rajvansha ka Itihasa* by Dr. D.C. Ganguli and Dr. Pritpal Bhatia's *The paramars* besides the work by K.N. Seth-*The Growth of Paramar Power in Malwa.* This Ph.D. thesis of Mrs. Ameta focuses on the regional history of Malwa.

The book is divided into seven chapters. The first chapter deals with the importance of Malwa as a geographical entity. It also makes the reader aware of the general history of Malwa with the coming of the Parmaras on the scene. The second chapter discusses the source material such as the inscriptions, coins, architectural remains and literature available for the study of the history of this dynasty. There is enough material for the political history of the Parmaras. In the third chapter the author gives the details of the administrative units and its administrators. The names of different inscriptions and land grants are given from page

53 to 82. In this chapter, description to various important cities and why and how they became important with the time are also found. The fourth chapter deals with the urbanisation of Malwa. The incentive of land grants inspired many of the *brahmins* who were well versed in the Vedas to come and settle down in Malwa. It is also stated that the religion besides the important trade routes played an important part in the urbanisation of Malwa. The author has taken pains in going deep into the study of the original names of some of the towns given in the copper plates, their exact location and then their present names and importance. In the chapter fifth, the author talks of different kinds of villages-villages which paid taxes and those which were exempted from such payments and the king generally donated those villages which did not fetch him any revenue. Thus there was no loss to the exchequer. She also gives details of weights and measures used at that time. In the sixth chapter, she discusses the importance of coins. She claims to have found references to coins issued by the Parmara kings as well which was denied by the earlier writers, of the history of the Parmars. The author tries to analyse as to why there was shortage of coins during this period, when and who inscribed these coins and the relationship of coins with the population of the state. In the last chapter, one finds the summary of the earlier findings.

No doubt, it is a well researched work but too many references to the inscriptions and their details which have nothing to do with the revenue system of the Malwas, make it at times, out of place. The new material with regard to the availability of the coins, why new coins were not inscribed and why the old ones continued and there was no loss of trade as stated by others adds to the importance of this work.

Saroj Gulati

INDIAN HISTORY AND CULTURE SOCIETY

Balance Sheet as on 31st March, 2001

Liabilities		Amount (Rs.)	Assets		Amount (Rs.)
Capital Fund			**Office Equipment**		
Op. Balance	195357.88		Op. Balance	160.00	
Add: L.M. Fees	16000.00		Less: Depriciation	24.00	136.00
Less: Excess of Exp.					
over Income	125.00	211,2320.88	**Furniture**		
			Op. Balance	106.00	
Donation for Books		100,000.00	Less: Depriciation	11.00	95.00
Current Liabilities			ICHR		45,000.00
Rajan Sharma & Co.		3,000.00			
Ch. K.S. Ramachandran		6,000.00	**Current Assets**		
Sh. K.N. Dikshit		17,500.00	S.B.I.-75148		311,788.37
Dr. S.P. Gupta		19,500.00			
			Cash		213.5
		357,232.88			**357,232.88**

Sd/- Vandana Kaushik
Organising Secretary

Sd/- K.N. Dikshit
Treasurer

In terms of our Audit Report of even date attached.
For Rajan Sharma & Co.
Chartered Accountant

Sd/- Rajan Kumar Sharma
(Rajan Kumar Sharma)
Pop., M.No.84457

Place : New Delhi
Date : 23.10.2001

INDIAN HISTORY AND CULTURE SOCIETY

Income & Expenditure Account for the year ended 31st March, 2001

Particulars	Amount (Rs.)	Particulars	Amount (Rs.)
To conference Expenses	50,792.00	By Delegation Fees	4,640.00
To Bank Charges	120.00	By Donation	27,000.00
To Conveyance Charges	2,400.00	By Grant for Seminar-ICHR	50,000.00
To Postage & Stamps	1,438.00	By Sale of Literature	2,697.00
To Printing & Starionery	1,916.00	By Grant for Publication (Amount receivable from ICHR)	40,000.00
To Professional Charges	1,500.00		
To Publication Expenses	63,261.00	By Excess of expenditure over Income	125.00
To Audit Fees	3,000.00		
To Depriciation	35.00		
	124,462.00		**124,462.00**

Sd/- Vandana Kaushik
Organising Secretary

Sd/- K.N. Dikshit
Treasurer

In terms of our Audit Report of even date attached
For Rajan Sharma & Co.
Chartered Accountant

Sd/- Rajan Kumar Sharma
(Rajan Kumar Sharma)
Prop., M.No. 84457

Place : New Delhi
Date : 05.10.2002

INDIAN HISTORY AND CULTURE SOCIETY

Balance Sheet as on 31st March, 2002

Liabilities		Amount (Rs.)	Assets		Amount (Rs.)
Capital Fund			**Office Equipment**		
Op. Balance	211232.88		Op. Balance	136.00	
Add: L.M. Fees	36060.00		Less: Depriciation	20.00	116.00
Less: Excess of Exp.					
over Income	958.00	246,334.88	**Furniture**		
			Op. Balance	95.00	
Donation for Books		100,000.00	Less: Depriciation	10.00	85.00
Current Liabilities			ICHR (Grant receivable)		15,000.00
Rajan Sharma & Co.		6,000.00			
Dr. S.P. Gupta		19,500.00	**Current Assets**		
Computer Associates		5,829.00	S.B.I.-75148		342,012.37
Dr. Vandana Kaushik		1,200.00	Cash		21,650.51
		378,863.88			**378,863.88**

Sd/- Vandana Kaushik
Organising Secretary

Sd/- K.N. Dikshit
Treasurer

In terms of our Audit Report of even date attached.
For Rajan Sharma & Co.
Chartered Accountant

Sd/- Rajan Kumar Sharma
(Rajan Kumar Sharma)
Pop., M.No.84457

Place : New Delhi
Date : 05.10.2002

INDIAN HISTORY AND CULTURE SOCIETY

Income & Expenditure Account for the year ended 31st March, 2002

Particulars	Amount (Rs.)	Particulars	Amount (Rs.)
To conference Expenses	60,335.00	By Grant for Seminar-ICHR	60,000.00
To Bank Charges	351.00	By Sale of Literature	4,493.00
To Conveyance Charges	2,700.00	By Grant for Publication	50,000.00
To Postage & Stamps	5,296.00	By Donations	23,500.00
To Printing & Starionery	4,320.00	By Excess of expenditure	40,000.00
To Publication Expenses	55,244.00	over Income	125.00
To Board Meeting Expenses	507.00		
To Establishment Expenses	200.00		
To Press Conference Exp.	6,968.00		
To Audit Fees	3,000.00		
To Depriciation	30.00		
	138,951.00		**138,951.00**

Sd/- Vandana Kaushik
Organising Secretary

Sd/- K.N. Dikshit
Treasurer

In terms of our Audit Report of even date attached
For Rajan Sharma & Co.
Chartered Accountant

Sd/- Rajan Kumar Sharma
(Rajan Kumar Sharma)
Prop., M.No. 84457

Place : New Delhi
Date : 05.10.2002

INDIAN HISTORY AND CULTURE SOCIETY

Balance Sheet as on 31st March, 2003

Liabilities		Amount (Rs.)	Assets		Amount (Rs.)
Capital Fund			**Office Equipment**		
Op. Balance	246,334.88		Op. Balance	116.00	
Add: L.M. Fees	23,060.00		Less: Depriciation	20.00	96.00
Less: Excess of Exp. over Income	90,356.00	179.038.88			
Dr. B.R. Grover Memorial Lecture Fund		150,000.00	**Furniture**		
			Op. Balance	85.00	
Donation for Books		100,000.00	Less: Depriciation	10.00	75.00
Current Liabilities			ICHR (Grant receivable)		15,000.00
Rajan Sharma & Co.		9,000.00			
Dr. S.P. Gupta		19,500.00	**Current Assets**		
Computer Associates		5,829.00	S.B.I.-75148		516,918.37
Vap Enterprises		19,659.00	Cash		1,542.51
Aquarelle		50,605.00			
		533,631.88			**533,631.88**

Sd/- Vandana Kaushik
General Secretary

Sd/- K.N. Dikshit
Treasurer

In terms of our Audit Report of even date attached.
For Rajan Sharma & Co.
Chartered Accountant

Sd/- Rajan Kumar Sharma
(Rajan Kumar Sharma)
Pop., M.No.84457

Place : New Delhi
Date : 21.10.2003

INDIAN HISTORY AND CULTURE SOCIETY

Income & Expenditure Account for the year ended 31st March, 2003

Particulars	Amount (Rs.)	Particulars	Amount (Rs.)
To conference Exp. (Ernakulam)	53,590.00	By Grant for Conff.	51,000.00
To Conference Exp. (Cochin)	1,556.00	By Sale of Publication	5,140.00
To Publication Expenses	70,264.00	By Delegation Fees	300.00
To Professional Charges	8,000.00	By Excess of Exp.	
To Conveyance	3,000.00	over Income	90,356.00
To Workshop on Fatehpur Sikri	6,167.00		
To Postage & Stamps	942.00		
To Audit Fee	3,000.00		
To Bank Charges	247.00		
To Depriciation	30.00		
	146,796.00		**146,796.00**

Sd/- Vandana Kaushik
General Secretary

Sd/- K.N. Dikshit
Treasurer

In terms of our Audit Report of even date attached
For Rajan Sharma & Co.
Chartered Accountant

Sd/- Rajan Kumar Sharma
(Rajan Kumar Sharma)
Prop., M.No. 84457

Place : New Delhi
Date : 21.10.2003

New Life Members

INDIAN HISTORY AND CULTURE SOCIETY

Shri Santosh Mehrotra
c/o Sudama Lal Omkar Saran
Doctor's Lane,
Rahemkhani Street
P.O. Kashipur
UTTARANCHAL-244713

Dr. Jyoti Marwah
Gyandeep, F1/5/1
Sector 3/4 Vashi
Navi Mumbai
MAHARASHTRA-400703

Ms. Anjula Kusum
E-19, Shastri Nagar
Meerut-250004
UTTAR PRADESH

Shri Sandeep Singhal
6191/1, BL-1, Dev Nagar,
Karol Bagh
NEW DELHI-110 005

Prof. Surekha Rajaram Sawant
Manish Nagar 28/315
'D' Wing, 4 Banglows
Andheri (W) Mumbai
MAHARASHTRA-400053

Ms. Rita Bhambi
A-702, Aalay Apartment,
Churiwadi, Goregaon (East),
Mumbai
MAHARASHTRA-400 063